The EMS Calling

A Path to a Purpose

By Brad Phillips, EMT-P

Copyright © 2025 by J. B. Phillips Sr.

All rights reserved. No part of this book may be reproduced, stored in a retrieval system, or transmitted in any form or by any means—electronic, mechanical, photocopy, recording, or otherwise—without the prior written permission of the publisher, except in the case of brief quotations used in reviews or scholarly works.

ISBN: 979-8-9989697-2-0 (Paperback)

ISBN: 979-8-9989697-1-3 (Hardcover)

Cover design by Brad Phillips All photos by Brad Phillips

Editing by Brad Phillips and Angie Bowen

Unless otherwise indicated, all Scripture quotations are taken from the New King James Version® (NKJV). Copyright © 1982 by Thomas Nelson. Used by permission. All rights reserved.

Scripture quotations marked NIV are taken from the Holy Bible, New International Version®, NIV®. Copyright © 1973, 1978, 1984, 2011 by Biblica, Inc.® Used by permission. All rights reserved worldwide.

This is a work of non-fiction. All stories, experiences, and insights shared within are based on real events and personal reflections. Some names and identifying details may have been changed to protect privacy.

For information or inquiries, contact J. B. Phillips Sr., Publisher

Theemscalling.com

Dedication

To my wife, Rhonda—
You've been by my side since we were kids. You are my one true love, a gift from God. Through every success and every failure, you've been my steadfast encourager, supporter, and friend. You've helped me stay grounded in my faith, and together we have grown as Christians. I can't imagine life without you, and I thank God daily for blessing me with you.

To my son, Joe—
God gave me one of the greatest gifts of my life when you were born. I've watched you grow into a humble man who lives to serve God and others. Despite the challenges you've faced, you've shown strength, resilience, and courage beyond your years. You've made me a better father and a better man. Whether you realize it or not, you are a constant source of inspiration to me and to many others. Always remember—I love you.

To my church family—
You have seen me grow from a child into a man. You taught me about Christ, pointed me toward salvation, and guided me through every stage of life. You've stood by me through baptisms, weddings, births, struggles, and celebrations. You've given me the opportunity to serve—leading worship, serving as a deacon, and walking alongside you in faith. Each of you at Buffalo Grove Baptist Church holds a special place in my heart.

To my Jefferson County EMS family—

To all those who have served past and present: we've shared the better part of three decades together. Like any family, we've laughed, argued, pulled pranks, celebrated life's milestones, and grieved great losses. We've stood side by side through unimaginable tragedy, answering the call to serve our community with compassion and professionalism. I am proud to have played even a small role among such a remarkable group of men and women. Never forget the sacred responsibility you carry—and never underestimate the difference you make every time you show up and answer the call.

Contents

Foreword	7
Introduction	11
Chapter 1: Follow your Heart	15
Chapter 2: Finding Compassion	21
Chapter 3: The Man in the Mirror	31
Chapter 4: Continually Fight Complacency	39
Chapter 5: Building Confidence and Commanding Calmness	47
Chapter 6: Bold, Brave, and Balanced	55
Chapter 7: Revealing His Vision	71
Chapter 8: Your Royal Court	81
Chapter 9. Firm, Fair, Flexible, Forgiving	105
Chapter 10: Next Man Up	125
Chapter 11: Point Man and Rear-Guard	137
Chapter 12: Dark Days and Defining Moments	147
Chapter 13: The Burdens We Bear	155
Chapter 14: The Seeds You Sow	167
Chapter 15: Wielding Your Sword	175
Chapter 16: No Investment, No Return	185

Contents Continued

Chapter 17: Ask, Seek, Knock   197

Chapter 18: Where Callings Intersect 207

Chapter 19: Finishing Strong   219

FOREWORD

It is a rare privilege to write a foreword for a book authored by someone who has been, for more than two decades, a trusted friend and a respected colleague, someone who has helped shape my path and my purpose. I first met Brad Phillips 25 years ago when I was serving as the Emergency Medical Services for Children (EMSC) Regional Coordinator at East Tennessee Children's Hospital. Over the intervening years, I have had the unique vantage point of watching him serve in many different roles—clinician, educator, leader, and servant of God—and in each he has demonstrated the same unwavering commitment to growth, both personal and professional.

Several years after we met, as I looked for ways to stay connected clinically in the prehospital world and maintain my own EMS skills, Brad welcomed me onto his team at Jefferson County EMS as a part-time paramedic. Brad provided me a new EMS home with knowledgeable, professional colleagues and a director who led with integrity. Years down the road, when life brought new challenges and I needed flexibility to care for an aging mother, he again extended an opportunity—this time to return to my first loves: EMS and pediatrics. By bringing me on as the Pediatric Emergency Care Coordinator for JCEMS, he not only gave me a role to fulfill, but restored a vital part of my identity and calling. For that, I am forever grateful.

In the high-stakes world of prehospital emergency medical services, leadership is not a luxury—it is a lifeline. Decisions are made in moments, lives hang in the balance, and character is revealed not in the comfort of strategy sessions but in the chaos of crisis. It is in this crucible that Brad has spent his career, not only providing patient care, but shaping the culture of care itself. Over the years, we've worked side by side on local, regional, and state committees and initiatives, always with the shared sentiment for improving care and strengthening leadership in prehospital medicine. And through it all, what has stood out most is not only his clinical ability or leadership acumen, but his unwavering faith that anchors every decision he makes. His leadership has always been marked by a resilient presence, a gift of discernment, and an unshakeable moral compass—all of which are grounded in his Christian faith.

This book is the culmination of a life spent both leading and learning. It is at once practical and profound, drawing from years of frontline experience and a deep well of spiritual conviction. Whether you're new to EMS leadership or a seasoned veteran, you will find in these pages not only guidance but inspiration—a call to lead with humility, purpose, and courage. Rooted in Christian principles and shaped by real-world experience, it offers wisdom, encouragement, and challenge to those who wish to lead or to grow in the leadership roles in which they already serve.

I've seen firsthand the difference Brad makes in people's lives, not only through the clinical care he has provided but through the example he sets. His passion for developing himself and others as leaders is contagious, and it has left an indelible mark on the JCEMS team and every other organization he has touched.

I am honored to commend this work to you. May it challenge you, equip you, and most of all, remind you that leadership—in EMS and in life—is not about titles or power, but about service, stewardship, and the steadfast pursuit of what is right.

Angie Bowen, MPS, RN, CPEN, NRP IC
Pediatric Emergency Care Coordinator
Jefferson County EMS
4 June 2025

INTRODUCTION

"Let nothing be done through selfish ambition or conceit, but in lowliness of mind let each esteem others better than himself. Let each of you look out not only for his own interests, but also for the interests of others."
Philippians 2: 3-4 NKJV

    As most people grow older, they begin to reflect on their lives and how they have lived. They seek to know what impact they may have had on the world and on the people who have crossed their path. We ask questions like: Did I accomplish my goals? Did I fulfill my purpose? Did I make a difference or a positive impact? These are common thoughts that run through our minds when we are facing a career change, a tragic loss of someone close to us, or any other life-altering moment.

    I suspect I am no different. I had passed my 30-year mark as a paramedic at Jefferson County EMS, nestled in the mountains of East Tennessee. Twenty of those years, I had served as the Director. I was considering if it was time to retire and where God wanted me next. I reflected and prayed about my life and what I had done with my God given gifts. My wife, Rhonda, had recently retired, after serving for 30 years as a Tennessee State Trooper which prompted me to consider my next steps also. On June 4, 2023, my 79-year-old mom died unexpectedly, and, by December 28th of that same year, my 82-year-old dad died from heart valve failure. This also pushed me to contemplate and evaluate my path and purpose.

I have always been a man of strong faith and have always tried to follow God's guidance in my life, to follow His path and fulfill His purpose for creating me. God gave this gift to me through my parents' example, how they lived their lives and what they taught me about Christ. As these life events coalesced, I began to reflect on the path God had placed me on and pray about where it was leading me next. I found that writing helped me work through my scattered thoughts. As I wrote out the words, they began to reveal to me how God had used me for his glory in some situations. I also reflected on the times I had failed Him, as well as those who depend on me, and thus the search for my next steps in His purpose continued.

Through this process it was revealed to me that my reflections of serving and leading others, the stories of success and failure, could possibly help someone else God had placed on a similar path, or possibly someone who was looking for their own God-given purpose in this world. So, I decided to put my thoughts and reflections in a format that I could share with others and see what impact it might have.

A quote credited to noted Christian author Max Lucado fits me perfectly and it says, "Throughout time God has often selected the most unlikely and unqualified people to do His work. He does this to show his handiwork. If we feel that we are qualified of our own doing then we risk thinking the accomplishments are all our own, but when we embrace our inadequacy, we are able to see it is God's handiwork and not our own."

    I certainly do not claim to be a writer, nor do I claim to be any type of expert on paramedicine or leadership. I would also never say that I know everything about religion. What I do know is that I have had a full and blessed life as a Christian, and a very rewarding career as a paramedic and as a leader in EMS. My hope and desire in writing this book is not to call attention to myself or anything that I have done, but to simply share my life experiences to highlight how God has used me for His purpose and that He may be glorified. The stories I share are of my life experiences and from my career as a paramedic and as a leader. They are not intended to place myself or any of my colleagues on a pedestal above anyone else. The stories are not shared to be glorified EMS tales that devalue the work of the dedicated professionals who have served, and continue to serve, in the EMS profession. I have served with the men and women of Jefferson County EMS for most of my career and any success I had is in large part due to their dedication and professionalism. While I do name several of my colleagues to add value to a story, it in no way takes away the importance of the work done by all who have worn our patch. I have worked with many dedicated professionals in other agencies as well who will go unnamed in this book, but it makes their work no less important or unnoticed either. There are thousands of skilled providers serving on the frontlines of EMS everyday making a positive impact on the people they care for. It is those who continue to silently serve that make this calling special.

The stories I share are from my own perspective and the lessons I learned from those experiences. I share them so that others may draw some knowledge from those experiences also. The specific details of many of the EMS stories have been slightly altered, or specific details left out, in order to protect the privacy of those involved. My prayer is that everyone who takes the time to read my thoughts and experiences, and how God used me to fulfill a small purpose in His great plan, finds something meaningful that may draw them to know God and help them find His purpose for their life in service to others no matter their profession. I pray that this book inspires you to learn and lead.

CHAPTER 1
Follow Your Heart

"Above all else guard your heart, for it is the wellspring of life" Proverbs 4:23 NIV.

I knew at a very young age growing up in my small country church that I wanted to help people in some way. As I grew older, I explored all kinds of options in my mind. I thought about becoming a missionary, a doctor, a teacher, a park ranger, or a soldier. I was searching for the way God wanted to use me and, of course, I had my own wants and desires that sometimes tried to take over. I knew God wanted me to follow Him, and my heart's desire was to make a positive difference in people's lives.

I was curious what talents I had to offer in God's service, and I was actively seeking what His plan was for my life. To add to that uncertainty, I lacked self-confidence. I was small for my age most of my childhood and did not see myself as worthy or capable of much. The one thing I was always confident in was that God had placed the desire to help others in my heart for a reason, and His Word promised that He would never forsake me and He would always walk with me.

I graduated high school in 1989 and had decided that I might be called to help people by becoming a nurse. I attended Carson Newman University where my mother worked as the secretary for the science department. That meant my tuition came at a huge discount because I would have never been able to afford that type of education otherwise. My grades and ACT scores were good enough to get me in. I enrolled in the challenging nursing program with a level of comfort given the amount of time I had spent going to work with mom during my summer breaks from school. I knew all the science professors and had helped them prepare labs and cadavers.

The thing I was not prepared for was the notable differences between a farm kid from the local town and the diverse group of students from all over the country who were primarily from more well-to-do families. I also didn't think about the fact that most of my classes would be with the other nursing students, and I was one of only two males in the program. Even though I was in my hometown, I still felt like an outsider. Additionally, I was not mature enough to be fully invested in my commitment to this educational pathway.

I had completed two and a half semesters in the program barely getting by and, quite frankly, I did not live up to my full potential. I was struggling to fit in with fellow students and was trying to figure out if this was really where God wanted me. My mom certainly had daily interaction with several of my professors in the science division and she certainly was not happy with my effort. I was feeling the pressure at school and the tension at home, so I decided to move out and share an apartment with one of my Walmart coworkers. I had been working at Walmart since graduating high school to support myself while attending nursing classes and I was trying to spread my wings. I completed the current semester and one additional semester before I decided to consider transferring to our local community college where I thought I might feel more comfortable. My prayer life during this time was not what it needed to be, and I was wandering aimlessly for a few months.

    I discussed the idea of transferring to the community college with my girlfriend Rhonda. She was attending there, studying for her degree in law enforcement, and could give me good advice about the college's atmosphere. Plus, I deeply valued her opinion. I soon decided to file all my transfer paperwork, send my transcripts, and try to enroll in their nursing program. What I discovered after talking with the program director is that there was typically a waiting list to get into their program but, since I had completed a significant portion of the course work, I could possibly jump ahead of others on the list. I would still have to wait through the upcoming summer semester to find out my status for the fall semester. The program director suggested I take a CPR class offered by the college's EMS instructors during the summer, and that would also help me move up the waiting list. I immediately enrolled in the CPR class, completely oblivious at the time how it would alter my plans but put me on God's path.

        It was in this basic class that I met the college's EMT instructor Larry Conner. He seemed passionate about teaching us skills that could save someone's life, and I began to ask questions about the EMT program. The more we talked, the more interested I became in this profession I had never really considered, as I had not had any interaction with EMTs or paramedics before. As I completed the class that summer semester, I found out that there was not going to be a spot for me in the nursing program that fall semester. Larry encouraged me to take the EMT class and I told him I would have to think about it. A friend of mine encouraged me to ride with one of the paramedics she knew to see what it was like. I got permission to ride along with Jefferson County EMS and had no idea what to expect. I was not like a lot of people in EMS who have family members in some type of public safety, so I came into it totally in the dark.

    I was able to ride a couple of shifts and I immediately fell in love with the profession. I saw the one-on-one interaction with the patients and the autonomy to make an immediate impact on people. With this new insight, I began to explore my options and talk to Rhonda, who encouraged me to pray about it and follow where God was leading me. I made the decision to put the nursing program on hold and begin the path to becoming an EMT and see where it would lead. To say the least, my mom was not exceptionally thrilled about the decision. It was hard to go against my parents when I knew they wanted the best for me, but I knew I had prayed about this and I was at peace that it was the right thing to do.

    I was working nights unloading trucks and stocking shelves and going straight to EMT class during the day. I spent most of my lunch breaks at work studying in a quiet corner of the store since there were no customers present while we were there. The EMT class material came easy for me. I suspect I had a leg up on some of the others because of the university classes I had already taken, even though my grades in nursing school were not the greatest. I was consistently scoring at the top of my EMT class and some of the other students were even reaching out to me for help. Larry began to encourage me and push me to be better. Learning the skills and riding clinical rotations on the ambulance came naturally to me, and it reinforced what I was feeling, and I was on the right track. Finally knowing this was where I needed to be, I was going to give every ounce of effort I had. Admittedly, I also wanted to prove my doubters wrong and prove to myself I could do it, but I also wanted to make sure I was doing my part because I could see God working through me and blessing me along the way.

    The key to following your heart is guarding it. The heart can be deceitful if you fill it with selfish desires; you will wander away from God's purpose in your life and begin to put self above God and everyone else. If you neglect your prayer life it will be difficult to hear God when He speaks to your heart to guide your steps. As human beings, and as leaders, we should try in all situations to evaluate our motivations when trying to achieve something. I usually ask the questions: Why am I doing this? Is this for my own benefit or recognition, or is it truly for the benefit of someone else? If it is solely for my own recognition, then I shouldn't do it. First, if I am being selfish, I am straying from the Christ-like principles of sacrificial servant leadership. He came into the world not to destroy it but to save it. Secondly, if I am seeking something out of my own selfish ambition, I am probably hurting or neglecting someone else I was meant to serve.

I am not suggesting we shouldn't have goals or desires. I am saying we should align those goals with the goals God has for us. He desires us to be our best, as that's why He created us. We each have a specific purpose in our lives and, as we grow older or we fulfill certain purposes, those assignments may change. However, God's path is always the right path. As stated in Matthew 7:13-14 NKJV, "Enter by the narrow gate; for wide *is* the gate and broad *is* the way that leads to destruction, and there are many who go in by it. Because narrow *is* the gate and difficult *is* the way which leads to life, and there are few who find it."

In a few short months after making this momentous decision, I graduated EMT class and immediately took the next step to become an EMT-IV. I found my calling, EMS, and my adventure in service to others began. I had guarded my heart, aligned it with God's plan, and began to follow it. Where it would lead, I had no idea, but I knew God would always be with me.

CHAPTER 2

Finding Compassion

"Let all bitterness, wrath, anger, clamor, and evil speaking be put away from you, with all malice, and be kind to one another, tenderhearted, forgiving one another, even as God in Christ forgave you."
Ephesians 4:31-32 NIV

    Mid-July in East Tennessee is notorious for being hot and humid, and this day had been exceptionally oppressive. My regular full-time partner was away on vacation, and this was my first time working with this particular new EMT. He seemed to be very bright and eager to learn, but he was very green and needed some coaching throughout the day. Nonetheless, we were getting accustomed to each other. We were standing outside the ER of our local hospital, trying to rehydrate a little after delivering them a cardiac arrest patient, an elderly female who had collapsed in her bathroom.

    Our resuscitation had been unsuccessful, primarily due to her age and comorbidities, but also due to lack of early CPR prior to our arrival. It had already been a busy shift, especially for a Saturday, as weekends were usually a little slower back in those days. It was approaching 2200 hours, we had not had the chance to eat supper, and we were both tired, sweaty, and hungry. We were quickly trying to clean our truck and get it back in service before all the restaurants closed.

I was running back in to get patient information from the admissions clerk when the dreaded tone went off again. I know I blurted out a choice word or two as I waited for the dispatcher to broadcast our next call. "Medic 3, Priority 1, MVA roll over" loudly echoed from the portable radio as I walked back to the ambulance and climbed in the passenger seat. Our response was quick, and we were the first emergency personnel to arrive on the scene. As we rolled up to the incident, I could already see a minivan lying on its passenger side in the ditch and a full-size Ford pickup truck sitting in the middle of the intersection with heavy front-end damage. I notified dispatch we were on scene and I requested they check on the availability of one of the helicopters in our area.

As we exited the ambulance, I started towards the minivan, since it had the potential for multiple passengers. I told my partner to check the truck and report what he found. I scrambled down the embankment, grabbed the mini–Maglite I carried in my cargo pocket, and crawled into the van through the back hatch that had popped open during the crash. I reached the rear seat first and my fears were confirmed as I found a 5-year-old boy in a broken booster seat. He was on the passenger side of the van that had taken the full impact of the truck, and that now was my floor from which to work.

I quickly assessed his airway, breathing, and pulse, but there were no signs of life in this crumpled little boy. I opened his airway and hoped for a breath...but nothing. I badly wanted to stop here and concentrate on this little guy but, as I looked closer, it was obvious his injuries were too severe to make survival likely. Additionally, I knew I had further triage to perform and currently had no additional resources on the scene. I quickly turned my attention to searching the rest of the van where I found an elderly female in the passenger seat with major head trauma and no signs of life either. The driver of the van was more difficult to locate, as she was apparently unrestrained and had been thrown into the floorboard of the passenger side, and the elderly passenger and items from the van had her obscured from my view at first.

Once I located her and crawled between the seats, I strained to reach her and check for any signs of life. She wasn't breathing and had no pulse, and I did my best to reposition her airway but to no avail. As I was exiting the crumpled van, I could hear my EMT yelling that he needed me at the truck. I told the arriving firemen that the three I had found in the van were all DOA and started climbing back up the bank to check on what my partner needed. When I made it to the pick-up, my partner had already applied a C-collar and O2, and I was impressed to see such initiative in a young EMT on such a bad call. The driver was the sole occupant of his vehicle and was trapped by the steering wheel and dash. I climbed in through the passenger window to better assess his injuries while the firemen prepared to begin extrication.

Once inside, the overwhelming smell of Jack Daniel's smacked me right in the face. I could see he was semi-responsive and had multiple severe injuries. I radioed dispatch to see if we had another ambulance coming to us and they advised the other two units on duty were already on emergencies; however, there was a helicopter in the air and on its way. As I continued my assessment, I could feel the anger and frustration begin to boil and rise to the surface as the fresh images of the van I had crawled out of, and the bruised body of the little boy and his family, flashed through my head. There were three separate generations lying dead in that van and here I was with this drunk driver who now needed me to treat his injuries.

He was intoxicated, agitated, and had no clue he had even been involved in a wreck, much less that he had killed three people. My anger and frustration with the whole situation continued to grow inside of me and I could feel myself wanting to deliver my own form of "street justice" as I reached in the jump bag for a needle to start his IV. In my head I told myself, "It's a trauma, I can justify this 14-gauge needle. It's dark and I am in a difficult position, so maybe if I miss a couple of sticks, nobody will question it." If you have never had a 14-gauge IV needle shoved in your arm, I suggest you don't ever experience it.

This guy had great veins, and I was confident I could get a 14-gauge easily on the first try but, inside my mind, I wanted to take a little retribution for the carnage he had caused. Ultimately, I really wanted to say screw this dude. I was about to shove the needle in his arm and something inside me said, "No, this is not you," and this time I listened. I regained my composure and started his IV on the first try. The fire department completed the extrication, and we moved the driver to the helicopter that had landed on the highway a few hundred feet from the accident scene. We handed the drunk driver off to the flight crew and I gave them a report on the patient and scope of the whole situation, and off into the night they went.

After they lifted off, we waited for the state troopers to finish their investigation and release the bodies to be transported to the local hospital until their family could be notified. We only had two body bags on our ambulance, which I used for the adults, so my only option was to wrap the little boy in a blanket. There were still no other ambulances available to help transport the bodies and, to be honest, at that point I wasn't going to let anyone else finish the call for me. We placed the mom on the bench seat and the grandma on the cot for transport. I sat down in the attendant seat holding the little boy in the blanket while my partner drove us to the hospital. I will never forget that lonely ride in the back of that ambulance holding that little boy in my arms and the rollercoaster of emotions I experienced that night.

Once we completed dropping the victims off at the ER, I returned to the ambulance to find the young EMT sitting on the bench seat in the back of the ambulance staring at the trash, dirt, and general mess we had created. I could tell he was struggling with something, so I climbed in and closed the doors and asked if he was okay. He said what most of us say in those moments, even if we don't truly mean it: "Yeah, I'm fine". I wanted him to know it was okay to talk so I began to share with him my frustration with the whole situation and how I really wanted to inflict a bit of retribution on that drunk driver for the lives he had destroyed. He looked up at me and asked me why I didn't deliver my "street justice" and why I worked so hard to take care of that guy. I told him, "It's tough, we don't get to choose our patients and we are certainly not the judge and jury", "This is what we do and it's not always going to be easy", and, "We are tools in God's hands and He is the ultimate judge on who lives and dies but He relies on us to do our best".

    I told the EMT that, despite that guy's poor choices, he is still a human being and deserves some form of compassion. I wanted this young kid to understand in this moment that it was okay to be angry, to have questions, and to be frustrated, but also that people need us regardless of the circumstances. Because we can't understand all of God's plans doesn't mean we can pick and choose who deserves our care. Furthermore, we have no way of knowing what God has in store for that drunk driver and his future. I also wanted him to know that, once the call is over, it's important to deal with our emotions in whatever healthy way works for each of us. Lastly, I wanted to convey to him how impressed I was with the way he handled himself on that scene and didn't delay taking appropriate action.

    We cleaned up our truck, went back in service, and made our way back to our station. Luckily that was our last call of the night, so we had the chance to talk a little more, obtain some food, and get some much-needed rest. The next morning, I told the young EMT to call me if he needed to talk and that, despite the tough day, I thought he had done an outstanding job, and I would be glad to work with him anytime.

The simple definition of the word compassion is the sympathetic concern for the suffering or misfortunes of others. You would think that in EMS, or in any other healthcare field, it would be a natural thing to be compassionate with our patients. After all, a large majority of EMS providers will tell you they got into the profession to "help" people and, naturally, that would require some level of compassion. Now granted, I could go deeper into the difference between compassion (sympathy) and empathy and how they work together, but there are numerous books already devoted to that subject. Simply put, compassion or sympathy is feeling sorry for someone's pain or situation whereas empathy is putting yourself in the other person's shoes and feeling and seeing the suffering from their perspective. It took me a long time to understand the difference between the two and how I needed them both to be a better paramedic and a better leader.

I usually didn't have much of a problem being compassionate and caring with my patients, as it came naturally to me to want to treat people with respect, and to feel "sorry" for them and want to help their situation. I had seen it modeled in my parents and in my church as I was growing up, and it was the Christ-like example I had been taught. On that hot, muggy July night with that drunk driver in the front of that truck, I struggled with finding the compassion that had been instilled in me. My anger over the senseless deaths, and my frustration with the absolute injustice, was drowning out the quiet voice of compassion in my heart. It didn't seem fair that three innocent lives had been taken away by the depraved decisions of a drunk driver and that he had survived his injuries and was not feeling much pain. Thankfully that night, I eventually listened to the small voice telling me to do the right thing, the compassionate thing.

EMS can be tough and extremely frustrating, and the more years we rack up, the more difficult it can be to hear the voice of compassion when she speaks. This is especially true in situations where the person we are there to help is belligerent, hateful, demanding, and seemingly ungrateful. We become calloused and thick-skinned, partially as a protective mechanism from the things we see and the tragedies we walk through. Compassion fatigue is a real thing and it's an infectious disease we must be vigilant to recognize and treat in ourselves. Don't misunderstand, I am not saying we must lie down and cry and get all touchy-feely emotionally with every patient on every call. Lord knows, and my colleagues will tell you; I am not the touchy-feely type anyway. I usually keep my emotions pretty close to the vest.

What I am saying is the best medicine that I have found for compassion fatigue is empathy. If I encounter a patient in the midst of their worst day, if an employee comes to me with a crisis, or if a member of my church is suffering, I can be more compassionate by being more empathetic. If we actively listen to the other person's problem while they are presenting it to us, and we place ourselves in their shoes, we can look at it through their eyes and we can begin to understand and respond in a more Christ-like manner. Have I always succeeded in finding compassion in every situation? That is an all-caps **"NO"**. We are each human, which means we are deeply flawed and often self-centered, seeing only how the situation is affecting us. We ask ourselves, "Why am I responding to this same house over and over to treat an overdose?", or "It's 2am and are they really calling us out because they have had a toothache for the past 3 days?" Sometimes you have been to the same residence over and over for lifting assistance for an elderly female in poor living conditions that you have reported multiple times, but the system keeps failing her. The employee who continues to struggle with poor decisions in their personal life keeps affecting their work performance and comes to you time and time again for help but continues to ignore your advice.

    I have, at times, struggled to find compassion and I have not always responded as I should have. I can tell you when I have responded poorly, I have walked away feeling defeated and, many times, have had to go back to those people and apologize. I can also tell you that the times I found compassion and responded with empathy, treating the person as I would want myself or my family to be treated, I felt accomplished and fulfilled, and I am certain everyone involved was better for it. Each new day is a gift, a chance to be better than we were the day before, an opportunity to make a difference in someone else's life. This is the privilege we have as EMS professionals and ours is one of several professions where our impact can become exponential. The compassion we show today can make a difference in someone's life. They might realize they are not alone, they feel they are cared for, it gives them hope, and it creates an opportunity for them to make an impact on their own. If we approach each day with the vision of God, and we listen to the still small voice inside of us, we will be able to find compassion and, thereby, change the world one person at a time.

The entire JCEMS Team, 2024

CHAPTER 3

The Man in the Mirror

"I will praise You, for I am fearfully and wonderfully made; Marvelous are Your works, and that my soul knows very well."

Psalms 139:14 NKJV

In addition to finding compassion for others, we must first be compassionate with ourselves. There have been many times I have looked in the metaphorical mirror and did not like what I saw. Research professor and author Brené Brown talks about this concept in her book "Daring Greatly". She talks about how often those of us who seek perfection, or perhaps have unresolved insecurities, often say things to ourselves in our minds that we would never say to someone else.

We must learn that we are enough and that we can never truly achieve perfection. It is better to be "in the arena daring greatly" than to be sitting in the bleachers waiting passively for the outcome. It has taken me almost my entire life to learn to love myself. From the insecurities of being a small kid, being told I was not good enough, and, at times, being bullied, I developed plenty of dislike for myself and acquired a lack of self-confidence.

By the time I reached adulthood, I had built a shield of protection, trying to overcompensate for my self-perceived inadequacies by projecting an air of over-confidence. This often came out as aggression, the so-called "little man syndrome". I can't tell you how many times my insecurities caused me to interact with, and respond to, people, even those close to me, in the wrong ways.

There were times I would lash out when I felt attacked. I reflect on the self-loathing things I would say to myself when things did not go as I thought they should, such as "You're an idiot!", "Why did you even try?", "Everyone knew you would fail.", and, "No one believes you can do this". In moments of self-doubt and insecurity I have said things to myself I would never say to someone I care about, and I have said them to myself in a tone that no human being should use with another human being.

A Story of Failure

One morning I received a call at my office, a complaint about the response and actions of one of my EMS crew members on an emergency call. I patiently took the complaint information and advised the caller I would need to investigate further, but I was certainly concerned by the details I had been given. I began by reviewing the run report, the 911 call log, and the ambulance vehicle tracking information to compare the times and data. The more I investigated, the less I liked what I discovered. I spoke to first responders from other agencies who were on the same call to get their version of the events. All the information I received not only verified the complaint information, but brought to light even more concerning details. I knew I needed to try and remain as objective as possible until I had gotten the employee's verbal statement on the incident in case there were details, they had failed to document in their written report. I did feel that if all the details I had been given were true in this situation, the decisions and actions of this employee luckily had not negatively affected this patient but, if repeated, could put lives at risk in the future. I knew this would need to be addressed immediately.

    I normally try to address performance issues with employees on their regularly scheduled work days, but this was potentially too severe an issue for me to wait. I called the crew member and asked them to come in that afternoon, telling them we had a significant problem and I needed further information. It was an employee I had counseled and coached on several occasions and, in a few instances, the infractions required disciplinary actions or suspensions. I am sure, given their past history, they knew it was not good I had requested them to come in on their day off, but they agreed to come and meet with me anyway.

    They arrived that afternoon and I invited them into my office. As a standard practice of mine, I included the on-shift supervisor as a witness to the conversation and as an additional leader to provide input and perspective if necessary. I proceeded to tell the employee about the complaint, that I had investigated some of the details, and that I wanted to get their statement on the events as they remembered them. I let them know I wanted to give them an opportunity to explain the details of the call and anything they may have failed to mention in the written report. They began explaining their version of the call and what they had seen and done. I listened closely, took notes, and asked clarifying questions.

Surprisingly, their version was very similar to what I had been told by other responders, but it was missing certain key facts. These were facts they had to know that I had access to from call logs, 911 tapes, and law enforcement body cams from the scene. The employee had purposefully left out key details they felt showed them in a negative light and that clearly violated our policies and procedures. As we were discussing the incident, I thought perhaps they had become so complacent they did not even realize the potential harm their decisions could have caused a patient. I told them that, as their leader, I had responsibility in their failure because I had not done an adequate job of coaching and mentoring them or helping them understand the impact their decisions have on their patients. While I had counseled them many times and tried to coach them on making better decisions in the past, yet here we were again and, this time, it was much worse and could have caused harm to the people we are here to serve.

I allowed them to finish their statement and answer all my questions before I began to express my concerns. I pointed out the dangers and risks to the patient that their decisions and inaction could have caused. I called them out on the details they had seemingly intentionally left out, and their lack of eye contact told me they knew I was correct. I asked them why they made the decisions they had made, and I got only excuses of how they did not see anything wrong with what they had done. I reiterated the issues and failures on this call, and I gave them every opportunity to tell me how they would change what they did and accept responsibility. But the more we continued, the more they shifted and denied any blame and refused to acknowledge their error.

One of the hardest parts of leadership is holding others accountable, and part of being a leader is the ownership you must take. When my team fails, it is ultimately my fault. I either failed to communicate the reason certain things need to be done in certain ways, or I failed to set clear parameters of operation. Perhaps I also failed to act soon enough and allowed bad behavior to go unchecked too long, thus lowering the standards of expectation. In this case, my failure to remove a problem employee sooner, choosing instead to repeatedly coach them up, could have led to harm of a patient.

Thankfully in this situation no harm did come to a patient, but it opened my eyes to the severity of the issues with this employee and I realized that they were no longer coachable. That meeting ended with the employee being terminated. It was not my first termination and, sadly, would not be my last. That list of terminations over my many years as director has woefully grown. It is what I refer to as my "leadership failures list" because losing an employee to termination traces back not only to the employee actions, but ultimately to leadership failures.

After that meeting, as with other similar employee encounters, I was very stressed and frustrated. The employee left, and I asked the supervisor to give me some time alone. I closed the door to my office and wanted to scream. I felt so defeated. I felt like crying. I told myself how stupid I was for not being able to correct the bad behaviors in this employee sooner. I told myself how inadequate I was as a leader for not being able to coach this employee up to our standards or get them the help they needed to resolve their personal issues. It brought back to the forefront a flood of other failures I had as a leader. I sat there for an hour or so internally beating myself up so badly that, if it had been actual physical wounds, I would have probably had two black eyes and a concussion. That self-degradation often creeps to the surface for me in situations such as this.

My wife, Rhonda, has been one of my biggest coaches and accountability partners as I have strived to improve this aspect of my life. We have been together since we started dating when I was 15 years old. I have often wondered what she saw in the hot-headed, blond-haired, blue-eyed boy I was back then. I have often questioned how I was so blessed that God placed her in my life. She was never afraid to hold me accountable when my emotions got the best of me, or when I did not respond appropriately to someone joking with me or teasing me in good clean fun. She put me in my place many times and called me out in my moments of excessive aggression during what were supposed to be friendly backyard sporting events. She pointed me back to God and His guidance in my life when I would neglect my relationship with Him.

With her help, I eventually learned that it all was rooted in a lack of love for myself and in my own feelings of inadequacy. She certainly saw something in me worth loving, and I should certainly love myself. God had created me according to His purpose and I was "fearfully and wonderfully made". How could I not love something God had created? Over time I learned to recognize the signs of self-hatred, anger, and aggression that would begin to bubble to the surface when I questioned my own abilities or performance. I began to see that I had a purpose, and that God had adequately gifted me for that purpose; therefore, as long as I was giving my best, it was enough. I needed to hold myself accountable, but I also needed to have compassion for myself and believe in myself more and more. I owe that self-confidence and self-love mostly to my wife. And while I am still far from perfect, I would not be anywhere close to the husband, father, or leader I am today without her understanding, patience, influence, and love. I should be her rock but, more often than not, she has been mine.

I still have times when I display confidence on the outside when, on the inside, I am secretly telling myself I don't have a clue what I am doing. Have all my insecurities gone away? No, and I don't think they ever will. I still have bouts of the dreaded "imposter syndrome". However, I have learned to recognize when these notions are trying to hijack my thoughts and pushing me to respond inappropriately. I have learned that even though the people I care about are counting on me in so many aspects of my life, they know I will never be perfect. They know my flaws and that, at times, I will fail them. They choose to love and accept me anyway and, consequently, I need to be compassionate with myself. This, in turn, helps me to be more compassionate with them. God has purposefully created each of us for His glory. As we stand looking into the mirror, we should always remember to honor God's creation that is staring back at us by loving and nurturing it, knowing that all God's creations are "marvelous".

CHAPTER 4

Continually Fight Complacency

"For the waywardness of the simple will kill them, and the complacency of fools will destroy them;" Proverbs 1:32 NIV

After the long hours I spent studying in paramedic school, I had grown tired of reviewing and reading. Additionally, my paramedic instructors and preceptors had done an exceedingly exceptional job of instilling confidence in me and, to be quite honest, I was way overconfident. I felt I was ready to change the world and thought I knew everything I needed to know about how to be a great paramedic. Of course, anyone who has been in our profession very long knows that this is a deeply flawed thought process and a very dangerous mindset. As the days turned to weeks and the weeks turned to months, I started to find myself becoming complacent about learning and developing myself into the best I could be. Many professions, but especially the EMS profession, are in a constant state of change. Therefore, if you want to be the best for your patients, you must keep learning; you must keep reading. If you add to my overconfidence the fact that I do not enjoy reading in the first place, I had a breeding ground for complacency. I know you are probably thinking, "if he hates to read, why is he writing this book?" Don't worry, I asked myself the same question several times, but still here we are.

I could feel the complacency beginning to take root but, with all the distractions of life, I was ignoring the weeds growing in my own garden. One chilly winter night at about 0200, my partner and I were snuggled in our warm, not-so-comfortable beds at station 1. Suddenly the silence of my slumber was broken by the awful ringing of the station telephone that sat right beside the head of my bed. This was a time before we had fancy tones to broadcast on the radio or other apps to dispatch us on the calls. If we were in the station, dispatch would simply call us on the phone when we had an emergency call. I was the lightest sleeper on my shift, so I was relegated to the bed closest to the phone.

I reached over, answered the phone, and heard the familiar voice of one of our dispatchers at the other end telling me we had a 2-year-old in respiratory distress, and she gave me the address. I rubbed my eyes, scribbled the address on the notepad, then kicked my partner's bed to make sure he knew we had a call and he needed to get up. We proceeded to put on our boots and gear up and went out the door. I knew the general area where we were going and knew our response would be short, so I didn't expect any updates on the patient before we arrived. And to be honest, back in those days, we rarely got updates while enroute anyway.

We arrived within about 5 minutes and proceeded down a long gravel driveway toward the faint glow of a porch light shining through the trees. As we pulled up to the front of the residence, my partner threw it in park and we both exited the cab to grab our equipment. We had been working together for a while, so we had our unspoken routine and roles down to an art form. I knew on this call that I would grab the airway bag and make first contact with the patient while he grabbed the monitor and stretcher. However, this time as I grabbed the airway bag and closed the compartment door, I heard footsteps behind me in the darkness. I immediately turned around to make sure it was not a threat, and I quickly realized it was the mother of our patient. I could see the fear and panic in her face as she approached the light given off by the scene lights on the ambulance. I dropped the airway bag to the ground as she handed me the lifeless body of the most beautiful 2-year-old little girl in pink princess pajamas.

It was immediately obvious to me that this was way more than the respiratory distress call that we had been dispatched to, and we now had a full-blown pediatric arrest. I was not prepared mentally for that moment of surprise, but that is EMS for you: expect the unexpected. To compound the surprise, you must remember I was in the midst of growing a garden of complacency and I hadn't run enough pediatric arrests to keep the drug dosages for these little ones fresh in my mind. You mix all that together and you have a recipe for a supersized stress burger with an extra helping of fear sauce, and I was about to take a huge bite from it. If I wasn't fully awake at first, I certainly was now.

I was cold, tired, surprised, unprepared, and fully lacking the usual self-confidence I had while on emergency scenes. Add to all that the fact that the whole time the mom is standing there with this look in her eyes that is forever burned into my memory; the look she had of sheer panic and fear coupled with the hope and expectation that I could fix her little girl. She was expecting my very best, and she deserved my very best, as she had handed me her most precious gift.

    If you aren't in EMS or you have never been in that situation or have never thought about it in that context, the weight of that type of responsibility is enormous. For someone to be vulnerable enough and trusting enough to put their faith in a total stranger amidst the worst day of their life is something I have never taken lightly. Yet there I was with all my sudden insecurities, hoping the mom couldn't sense or see the lack of confidence I had in myself, as I took her little princess in my arms and leaped up into the back of the ambulance. Once I got inside my truck, I began to feel more like myself because now I was in familiar territory where it was well-lit and warm, and I knew I had everything I needed within arm's reach. I caught myself taking a deep breath to calm myself but also to get some oxygen back in my body, as I had unknowingly been holding my breath for a few seconds.

    My training quickly took over and my partner and I began trying to breathe life back into this precious angel on our stretcher while we waited for a fireman to arrive to drive us in. Thankfully my service had prepared for such a moment as mine, and they had additional tools to help us with drug dosages and equipment sizes. We worked to the best of our ability, utilizing everything at our disposal, all under the watchful tear-filled eyes of the mother. I had intubated this little girl's tiny airway successfully on the first attempt and continued ventilations while my partner performed chest compressions. Then we continued to perform all the other ALS interventions during the emergency transport to our regional children's hospital about 30 minutes away.

    Once we arrived at the ER, we handed our patient over to the nursing staff with a faint pulse and a critically low blood pressure, but she still showed no signs of breathing on her own. As I finished giving them my handoff report, took off my gloves and turned to exit the room, the mom grabbed me and hugged me to thank me for helping her daughter. I gave her my typical answer of, "That's what we are here for", "Your daughter is great hands now", and "You will be in my prayers", and then I was off to clean my truck. The whole time she was hugging me, and the entire walk out to the ambulance, I was secretly hoping she couldn't tell how doubtful I was about the prognosis for her daughter and how inadequate I felt as a paramedic at that moment.

    I knew that my partner and I had done everything any other paramedic crew would have done, and that we had given all the right medications and treatments, but my self-doubt was still eating at me. I knew I was not as prepared as I should have been, I knew I had allowed the seeds of complacency to take root in my garden and it had yielded its first fruits of mediocrity, and I didn't like how they tasted. It was a small but intense dose of inadequacy, and I didn't like how it felt. I knew I was lucky that this call hadn't gone more poorly or, even worse, allowed me to cause harm to the patient. I didn't desire, nor did I want to become, a mediocre paramedic. I had seen, and even worked with, a few in the past so I knew what the fruits of those seeds would yield if allowed to multiply. I have always held a high standard for myself and, that night at the back of that ambulance, I made a promise to myself to never be in that place of complacency again. Patients' lives depended on me being at my best and the ability to fulfill my purpose depended on me being at my best.

Obviously, I still think about that night, as I do many other calls in my career. I still see the fearful, tear-filled eyes of that mother. I can see the pink pajamas of that little girl. I remember the feeling of inadequacy and failure. Even though I know the outcome that night was not what anyone wanted, I know that ultimately it was beyond anyone's control. After all these years I still can't answer why these things happen, but I do know that this call made me a better paramedic and, eventually, a better leader.

Fighting complacency in any part of our life must be a consistent part of our daily routine. As an unattended garden will quickly be taken over with weeds, our lives can quickly become overwhelmed with complacency. We can become complacent in our professional lives, our spiritual lives, our marriages, and our other relationships. The deeper the roots of complacency grow, the faster the seeds of mediocrity begin to spread to other parts of our life and then they begin to permeate everything. The longer it's allowed to progress, the harder it is to root out.

As leaders, we must be self-aware regarding our own tendencies to become complacent, and we must be intentional about self-improvement and growth. We need to study our craft as EMS providers and as leaders. We need to read respected authors and the principles put forth by other leaders. We need to attend conferences, listen to podcasts, and network with others in our field, utilizing every tool available to become better. Also, as leaders we must identify that same complacency in those we lead and find ways to motivate and encourage them to be proactive in their own growth. We must cultivate a culture of continuous curiosity and learning, a place where a healthy unhappiness with the status quo is encouraged. The overall success of our lives, our people, and our organizations depends on us being at our best. And, in a field like EMS, others' lives very much depend on us being at our best. King Solomon wrote in Proverbs; complacency is a fool's venture that will ultimately lead to destruction. Therefore, it is our God-given duty to continually fight complacency in our lives and in our organizations.

CHAPTER 5

Building Confidence and Commanding Calmness

During my first few months at Jefferson County EMS, while I was working to finish paramedic school, I was lucky enough to be assigned with my mentor and prior paramedic partner from Grainger County, Don Gass. Don had two full-time jobs for quite a while, at Grainger County EMS, where we first worked together, and Jefferson County EMS, where he helped me get hired. He had a great deal of experience that he shared, and I learned a lot from him. We had built a strong friendship and had become a polished team, and I cherish those days we had together.

As life would have it, after I finished paramedic school, the JCEMS Director, had received funding to add additional shifts, and he reassigned me to partner with another new paramedic. His name was Mardy Bowen, and he and I started working on building a relationship and figuring out our routine on calls. Mardy had only graduated from paramedic school six months before I did; however, he did have more experience as an EMT, so I knew I could rely on him and I hoped he knew he could rely on me. I had finished at the top of my paramedic class, which helped build my confidence in my abilities, but it certainly helped that I was working with another paramedic while trying to become one myself. This same confidence also enabled me to be calm under pressure and, over time, I came to realize this was one of the gifts God had given me to help me travel this path and ultimately fulfill his calling in my professional life.

One day Mardy and I were at station 1 when we received a call for a motor vehicle crash in town. We responded priority 1 and the other truck at that station said they would roll our way non-emergency until we knew what we had. As we rolled through the city intersections, we received word from dispatch that there was confirmed entrapment and multiple patients. When the dispatcher made this confirmation, the crew on the other truck, Tim, an EMT at the time, and Robin, a seasoned paramedic, upgraded to emergency traffic. As Mardy and I arrived at the scene, we encountered a car with heavy front-end damage sitting in the middle of an intersection. It took Mardy and I a few seconds to notice the second car, as it had been hit so hard it traveled off the highway and down a small embankment into the parking lot of a nearby shopping center. A large crowd was already gathering in the parking lot and frantically waving for us to pull down there. I called Tim and Robin over the radio and told them to check on the car in the roadway and we would take the car in the parking lot with severe damage.

Once we got out of the ambulance, we found two male passengers in critical condition. Mardy went to the driver and I went to the passenger. Mardy was able to free the driver with assistance from firefighters and move him to the ambulance. On the passenger side, the car had intrusion so severe it had pushed the passenger seat all the way to the center console. As I crawled in to better treat my patient, he quit breathing but still had a faint palpable pulse.

Tim was taking care of the driver at the intersection and Robin was making his way down to check on me, as I was in the crumpled compact car straddling my patient and starting to ventilate him with a bag-valve-mask (BVM). Jeff Coffey, one of our police officers who was also a paramedic, was outside the passenger window asking me what I needed so he could hand it to me. At this point, Jeff and I had never worked on any EMS calls of significance together, so I don't think he knew my capabilities or was very sure about me as a young new medic. I am certain he had no idea what to expect from me on this severe call.

I looked out the passenger window and told Jeff I was going to try to intubate the patient and I needed a laryngoscope and endotracheal tube. Jeff seemed to hesitate for a second, as if to question if I could actually intubate this guy while I was literally sitting nose to nose with him in this crumpled car.

While I was preparing the patient for this difficult intubation, the firefighters were working to cut the roof off the car. Thankfully my instructors in paramedic school had the foresight to run us through a similar scenario of intubating a patient while in a confined space, a procedure referred to as the "claw hammer" technique. This was one of my most critical calls since graduating paramedic school and now I had Jeff and Robin, two experienced paramedics, standing outside the car watching my every move.

Jeff handed me the items I needed, and he asked if I was sure I could do this. Robin, being a bit high-strung, was outside the driver's window the whole time telling me to tube this guy or get out of the way. I did my best to block all the noise and ignore the distractions around me, and I focused on the task at hand while relying on the training I had received. Thankfully, I was able to intubate the patient on the first attempt. Robin helped me secure the tube in place and I continued to ventilate my patient. I am pretty sure I saw a bit of surprise on both Jeff's and Robin's faces because I had been able to complete such a difficult task. And, to be honest, I was a bit surprised myself.

The firefighters removed the roof of the car, fully exposing myself and my patient, but also giving me more room to work. Robin was starting an IV as I took a moment to look around. I came to the realization we now had an audience of at least 50 people watching us work as we tried to save this young man. The firefighters continued to work to free the young man's legs and Robin completed the IV. As I began to formulate a plan to move the patient once he was freed from the wreckage, I noticed something very strange. There were no longer any ambulances on our scene.

My partner Mardy had commandeered one of the firemen to drive him to the landing zone at the hospital so he could get his patient on the way to the trauma center. Tim had recruited another fireman to drive him to the hospital, transporting the driver from the other car who only had minor injuries. I looked at Robin and Jeff and asked, "WHERE did our ambulances go? Please tell me that the other ambulance crew is on their way from station 2." Robin got on the radio and the dispatcher confirmed the other ambulance was about 5 minutes away to help us transport our patient.

As a paramedic, it is a chilling thing to look up and realize that you do not have your ambulance. For us it is our safe space, it is where all our tools and supplies are, it is the most critical part of moving our patient to definitive care. We fortunately had all the equipment we needed to treat our patient on the scene while we waited for the Medic 2 crew, Don and his wife and EMS partner Charlotte, to arrive. Once there, we loaded our patient and transported him to the hospital. Sadly, I later learned he eventually succumbed to his injuries.

Through all the chaos, the onlookers, the noise of the extrication, and the fact I had no ambulance for a few minutes, surprisingly I had stayed relatively calm. I had leaned on my confidence in my training and my skills, and I knew I was prepared and capable of handling the situation. I innately knew this was what God created me for; this was a moment in which I was meant to be present and use my gifts. I built even more self-confidence that day and I think I also earned the respect of Jeff and Robin. I was secretly hoping that now they would trust me even more as a paramedic on future calls.

I was never cognizant of the finer details regarding what was going on around that scene because I was so focused on the patient and the difficult circumstances in which we found ourselves. However, several days later I ran into one of my friends from high school who said he saw me at that wreck. He saw me working in that car, frantically trying to save that young man's life. I told him I never noticed him in the crowd, but that was certainly a crazy call. My friend proceeded to tell me how surprised he was that I was so calm during such a bad situation, especially with all the people standing around watching every move we made. He said what a lot of people say to those of us in EMS: "I don't see how you do it!" I told him that I had good teachers who trained me well but, most importantly, God had gifted me with the confidence and the calmness to do this work.

Confidence in ourselves and our abilities is extremely important. It enables us to perform at our best, to look forward and press through difficulties. If we focus on our failures or weaknesses too much, it may cause us to shy away from a critical task or to fail to step up during a crisis. We risk succumbing to the paralysis of fear. We build our confidence through practicing our skills, studying new medical research, and taking refresher courses. It's analogous to a professional basketball player who continues to shoot thousands of shots per week in practice even though he is the leading scorer on his team, or a major league baseball player who takes hundreds of pitches in the batting cage despite having the highest batting average in the league. EMS professionals need to continually hone our craft, increasing our confidence which, in turn, helps create calmness in the midst of a crisis.

However, as is true with many things, too much of something good can become bad. Confidence that grows into arrogance is a recipe for disaster. Whether you are a field provider or an executive leader, becoming overconfident or conceited will open you up to failure. It makes us less observant and less self-aware. It causes us to miss key details or have tunnel vision regarding our own ideas, thereby failing to see a problem or even a hazard. We set up not only ourselves, but also our team, for failure if we become blinded by our own vanity and respond to situations as if we are incapable of making mistakes. It is a fine line we walk between having enough confidence to act amid chaos without freezing and being self-aware enough to know we are not perfect and working to mitigate any potential pitfalls. We must ensure we stop short of stepping from quiet confidence into arrogant conceit.

Whether the paramedic on the scene of a major crash with multiple things going on around you, or the lead medic on a cardiac arrest in the dark hallway of a single-wide trailer, your calmness, or lack thereof, will be contagious. If you can keep your cool during the commotion, the temperature of that scene, and consequently of your fellow responders, will mimic yours. If you are running around like your head is on fire, your actions will raise the stress level of everyone else and the tone of the whole call will go in the wrong direction. The same is true for those in leadership. Those we serve and lead are watching how we respond to stressful events and will often follow our example. We are the tone setters, especially during a crisis.

I have been blessed with a strong sense of calm in my life, and I draw that from God and the assurances I have from Him. **Romans 8:28** NKJV assures us, "And we know that God works all things together for the good of those who love Him, who are called according to His purpose." God also tells us in

Philippians 1:6 NKJV, "...being confident of this, that He who began a good work in you will carry it on to completion until the day of Christ Jesus." I draw from Him the calmness in the storm and carry those assurances with me wherever I go, no matter the circumstances I face.

    I am often told by my friends, my coworkers, and my colleagues from other agencies that they appreciate the fact that I do not get excited in stressful situations. They tell me they have often felt calmer and safer because of how my reactions and demeanor changed the trajectory of the storm. This calmness is one of the things that has afforded me success as a paramedic and as a leader. I built my confidence by recognizing complacency in the practice of my profession and working to avoid it. I have strived to remain self-aware, keeping my arrogance in check (most of the time) and doing my best to avoid the dreaded "paragod" syndrome. I have drawn from my confidence and have chosen to command calmness when faced with any calamity. It has served me well and, if you learn the art of building your confidence in yourself and remaining calm in the face of adversity, you too can be successful in fulfilling your purpose and calling. Those around you will draw from your strength and resolve no matter the occasion.

CHAPTER 6
Bold, Brave, and Balanced

"For God has not given us a spirit of fear, but of power and of love and of sound mind." 2 Timothy 1:7 NKJV

The world can be a scary place. Some of our fears are quite rational and real, while others are exaggerated and baseless. For example, the fear of dying in a car crash is quite rational given that these events happen every day, especially if you drive significant miles as part of your job. However, while the fear of drowning in a vat of chocolate syrup might be rational for "Willy Wonka", it is highly unlikely if you do not work in, or ever plan to visit, a large-scale chocolate factory. In EMS, some of our rational fears are being struck while on the scene of a car wreck, being killed in a crash while running emergency traffic, or even being shot or stabbed to death by a violent patient. However, the fear of being trapped by falling debris in a "hoarder house" and no one finding you, while possible, is highly unlikely and somewhat irrational. Certainly these are extreme examples of the fears we must fight against, but the most common fear we must face is the fear of failure.

The fear of failing is an invasive thought process that can easily consume us and hold us back from achieving our potential. It can stunt our individual and spiritual growth, and inevitably rob us of our opportunity to fulfill our purpose. We hold ourselves back and choose not to take the chance, especially when the task we face is challenging and we feel inadequate. As touched on in the Building Confidence and Commanding Calm chapter, we can become paralyzed by fear and never have the courage to act. In our personal lives we face many struggles and challenges, whether in our relationships, with our health, or related to our finances. In our professional lives we face many performance and advancement challenges. As a leader, the challenges exponentially increase as our responsibilities and our obligatory number of decisions multiply. Any decision or challenge we face will require us to be bold, brave, and balanced. We will explore each of these traits throughout this chapter.

Before my first supervisory role forced me to abandon it, I had the opportunity to fulfill a personal dream by becoming a flight paramedic for an aeromedical service in our area. I applied for a part-time position for some secondary employment to supplement my salary, but primarily I hoped to expand my skill set and chase my dream. I admit this is one of the times I did not fully seek God's guidance to see if this is where He wanted me, but He allowed me to divert down this path even though He had other plans.

As part of my field orientation, I was required to go on several flights as a third crew member to be observed by an experienced flight nurse and flight medic. Their job was to educate me on the safety procedures, equipment, and protocols, as well as observe how I performed on those flights, before I could be released to work with my own crew. While on duty for what would be my last orientation shift, we received a request from a small hospital in Kentucky for a critical patient to be transferred to a higher level of care. The pilot performed his mandatory weather check, plotted our flight path, and made sure all factors were suitable to accept the flight. We all agreed the conditions were good and made our way out to do our pre-flight safety checks. We loaded into our Bell 407, which has been a workhorse in the aeromedical field for some time. It is a smaller airframe and is a bit cramped for space, especially with an extra crew member. The pilot fired up the engine and we soon lifted from the helipad and headed north to Kentucky.

It was a beautiful clear blue day with not a single cloud in the sky, and the fall colors were at full peak as we crossed the Cumberland Mountains. I was taking it all in and enjoying the smooth ride, admiring the sheer beauty of God's creation below on what was to be about a 40-minute flight. The lead medic got my attention on the headset when he told me this flight was going to be my "show", which meant I was going to take the lead so they could see how I performed. This brought me back to reality from only being a tourist taking it all in. I started dialing in my thoughts and going over potential scenarios in my head to help me prepare and refresh my memory on everything that would require my focus.

We landed safely in the secured parking lot of the hospital and prepped the equipment we would take inside. Meanwhile the pilot shut down the helicopter, as this was a cold load situation. Hospital security escorted us into the hospital and to the patient's room. As we approached the room, there were a couple of nurses standing outside in the hallway and I could tell by their facial expressions that something was not right. They each had a look of desperation on their face, coupled with signs of relief that we were finally there. As we entered the room, we encountered two additional nurses, a physician, and a respiratory therapist who was actively providing ventilatory support for the intubated patient. I asked the flight nurse to begin looking through the paperwork and setting up our IV pumps while I asked the physician for report on the patient's diagnosis and treatment.

    The physician told me the patient had suffered a hemorrhagic stroke, was deteriorating, and was unable to control his airway to the point of requiring intubation. He stated the intubation had been difficult, but he was able to successfully complete it on the third attempt. He proceeded to inform me that, despite the intubation and 100% oxygen, the patient's oxygen saturation was still only 94%. This caught my attention, and I could tell by the facial expression and body language of the respiratory therapist that something was off. The physician completed his report and said he needed to step out of the room for a minute but would be right back.

I took this opportunity to have the other medic take a quick peek at the chest x-ray for tube placement confirmation. It showed the tube was in the proper location, at least at the time of the x-ray. I utilized my stethoscope and checked breath sounds while the respiratory therapist ventilated the patient. The breath sounds were equal bilaterally but seemed diminished. I next checked the tube and the other equipment. The pilot balloon on the tube was flaccid, which indicated the distal cuff of the tube was not fully inflated. I looked at the respiratory therapist and she directed me to put my hand near the patient's mouth. I could feel air each time she ventilated the patient, which further confirmed that the distal cuff was not functioning properly. She whispered in my ear that she thought the physician had torn the cuff while trying to insert the tube, and I agreed with her assessment of the possible problem.

The physician reentered the room and saw that the respiratory therapist and I were discussing the problems with the tube, and I was attempting to reinflate the distal cuff. He did not seem happy with us implying there may be problems with his intubation. I informed the physician that I felt I needed to change the tube to better benefit this patient and to avoid any problems during our flight. It is an understatement to say he did not take it well.

I was now in a precarious situation. I was standing in his facility speaking to a provider who held a higher level of licensure. It was still ultimately his patient, but I had an obligation to advocate on behalf of this patient. The lead medic stepped out of the room to let our pilot know it was going to be a little longer than we anticipated. The doctor proceeded to tell me that if I removed the tube he placed, he did not think I could successfully reintubate. He stated that it was currently still his patient and we needed to load the patient and get going.

I knew the patient needed a new tube but I also knew that, ultimately, if I pushed the envelope too far with this physician, he may decide to not let us transport the patient. That decision would be definitively worse for the patient. I stepped into the hallway as if to check some equipment, but I really wanted the opportunity to discuss my plan with the lead medic and nurse. I told them I felt if I pushed too hard on the tube issue, the physician might cancel the transfer, which this patient obviously needed, but that the patient definitely needed a new tube. I told my crew the patient seemed stable enough at the moment and, once we got to our helicopter, the patient was definitely ours and I would reintubate in the aircraft prior to takeoff. They agreed that this was not the norm, that reintubation in the aircraft was not the optimal plan, but it appeared to be the only option given the resistance of the physician to any other alternatives. They also agreed with my assessment and plan, as long as I felt confident and I could mitigate the inherent risks.

We reentered the room and told the physician we would prepare the patient for transport in his current state. Once we had the patient prepped and ready for flight, the nurses and the respiratory therapist assisted us in rolling the patient out to the aircraft. While on our way out, I assured the staff that we were going to take good care of the patient and I would change the tube once in the helicopter. They were very appreciative, even relieved, and apologized for the physician's behavior. Once the patient was on board and secured, I climbed into the medic seat at the head of the patient and closed the doors. The lead medic and nurse climbed in the other side, and we began preparing the patient to change out the tube while the pilot prepared the aircraft for our flight back to Tennessee.

I was nervous. I was about to remove a tube I knew was in place and through which I was able to ventilate, but I also knew it was not functioning at its full capacity nor was it going to be effective in protecting the airway of this patient if he vomited. Add to that nervousness the comment from the physician that he did not think I could successfully intubate this patient. I had now compounded the stress by electing to perform this in the aircraft with limited space to work and with the patient's head sitting practically in my lap. I knew deep down that this patient needed a new tube, and I had to be bold enough and brave enough to do the right thing.

I double-checked that we had everything we thought we would need to change this tube, I hyper-oxygenated my patient, took a deep breath for myself, and pulled the existing tube from the patient's airway. I quickly inserted the laryngoscope, located my landmarks, and easily advanced the new endotracheal tube into its proper position and inflated the distal cuff. My lead medic gave the patient a couple of ventilations, and I then double-checked to confirm placement. I instantly knew that I had successfully changed out the tube and it was functioning properly. I breathed another sigh of relief, and the lead medic told the pilot we were good for start-up and lift-off whenever he was ready. The remainder of the flight was uneventful, and we delivered the patient safely without any complications to the receiving facility.

Once we cleared and prepared to fly back to base, the nurse patted me on the back and told me she couldn't believe I was brave enough to change that tube given how new I was, but she thought it was the right call. The lead flight medic told me he probably would have pushed a little harder with the physician, but he understood my reasoning and, ultimately, he was glad I was bold enough to express my concerns and eventually take the calculated risk for the betterment of my patient. After that shift was complete, the lead medic informed me he would be submitting the paperwork for my required field training to be complete.

Being Bold

"Now, Lord, look on their threats, and grant to Your servants that with all boldness they may speak Your word," Acts 4:29 NKJV

Boldness is often described as the courage to speak or act without fear of real or imagined dangers. When we act boldly, we step up or speak up regardless of the risks. Boldness was one of the first gifts received by Jesus' disciples from the Holy Spirit after Jesus' ascension into Heaven. Jesus had been crucified, buried, and rose from the dead. He then appeared to the disciples and multitudes of people over the course of 40 days after his resurrection. Before ascending into Heaven, He instructed the disciples to remain together in prayer and He would send them the Holy Spirit to give them power to become witnesses for Christ to all the earth.

We read in Acts chapter 2 that, on the Day of Pentecost, the disciples were in one place and of one accord. Almighty rushing wind filled the whole house and they each received the Holy Spirit, giving them the ability to speak in many of the varying languages of the world. With this newfound gift, they immediately began to witness to the multitudes of people in their native languages, telling of the salvation that Jesus offered.

Emboldened by the spirit, they began to go out daily preaching and performing miracles in Jesus' name. They had been witnesses to what the Jewish leaders had encouraged the Roman rulers to do to Jesus during the crucifixion. They had to know that the Jewish leaders would not like them preaching about Jesus' resurrection and offering the redemption of God to all people. As word began to spread, they quickly came under threats of prison, torture, or death. It was under these conditions of persecution and threats that Peter and John prayed for boldness and received it.

Because of their boldness, thousands received the promise of salvation through Jesus Christ. Their early concerns and fears proved to be rational, as eventually each of them was killed for preaching the Gospel, but their boldness set in motion the exponential growth of Christianity and the spread of God's Word. As Christians, we should pray for this same boldness to go forth and proclaim the salvation through Christ alone, using that boldness to overcome our fears of rejection or persecution. We are each called to be witnesses for Christ so that others might be saved.

      As paramedics, we are on the frontlines of healthcare and our number one responsibility is to be a patient advocate. When we have a patient experiencing self-neglect or needing medical care, but who is refusing treatment, we must be bold enough to speak up and take time to compassionately explain why further care is essential. If we encounter a vulnerable patient who we feel is in a dangerous or abusive situation, we have a moral and legal obligation to be bold and report our concerns. When we encounter a patient who needs corrective intervention or correction of care from another medical provider, like my earlier example, we must be bold enough to respectfully express our concerns on behalf of that patient. While I did speak up to the physician in Kentucky, I could have been even more bold than I was and possibly mitigated the risks even further. Each is entitled to their opinion as to how far I should have pushed that situation. As I reflect on it, I should have been firmer with my concerns and pushed them to perform the intubation in the more suitable hospital environment.

      As a leader we will often be put in situations where we need to be bold. When an employee is underperforming or not meeting the standards of the organization, we need to be bold enough to intervene and hold that person accountable. When we identify a potential safety issue with a piece of equipment or a process, we must be bold enough to call attention to the issue and take immediate action to address and correct it. When our agency or department has a critical financial need, or we need approval from the governing board or officials for a critical project, we must be bold enough to present our request. When our agency comes under public scrutiny or unjust attack, we must stand up for our department without fear of retribution, ridicule, or, in a worst-case scenario, removal from our leadership position.

We must proceed without fear when the cause is just, and we must make a stand to make things better for our fellow man. That begins with sharing the good news of salvation without fear of rejection. It continues with our service to others and advocacy for those who cannot advocate for themselves. Our boldness must be balanced and tempered as to not be perceived as pushy, aggressive, or overly confrontational. Our boldness should never push us into taking unnecessary risks or accepting a dare to prove we can do something. Without discerning judgment, our boldness can lead to precarious behavior or hurtful words. Our boldness must always come from a place of love for others and, if it is, it will always be demonstrated in the appropriate way.

Being Brave

"Have I not commanded you? Be strong and of good courage; do not be afraid, nor be dismayed, for the LORD your God is with you wherever you go." Joshua 1:9 NKJV

Some often confuse boldness and bravery as the same thing. While they often go together, there are distinguishable differences, and we need both characteristics in our lives. As I have already discussed, boldness is about taking calculated risks, knowing the potential consequences, and being assertive. Bravery, on the other hand, is more commonly associated with showing courage in the face of adversity. In other words, boldness requires us to act while bravery is more reactive, such as the ability to endure a hardship or attack. We see bold individuals as those who stand on their principles and are willing to speak up in defense of those principles. Individuals to whom we attribute bravery are those who face challenges head-on despite any fear they may have. Those who are brave usually do not seek risky situations; however, they are typically willing to confront any challenge that may arise.

As Christians we draw our source of bravery from the strength and promises of God because He promises to be with us every step of the way. Joshua faced the daunting task of replacing Moses and leading the Israelites into the promised land, but God told him on several occasions to be "strong and courageous". God knew the formidable enemies Joshua and Israel would face as they established themselves in the new land. Because of God's promise to always be with him, Joshua could be brave and move forward with confidence. We as Christians have that same promise, that God will never forsake us nor will He fail us. He is a loving and sovereign God who is always working for our good. This does not mean we will never face adversity, sickness, or danger, but He promises to be with us and strengthen us. Therefore, we can bravely face anything if our faith is in Him.

As paramedics we face dangers and fears over the course of our careers. Bravery is simply the act of facing that fear, being capable of overcoming it, and doing what needs to be done. Let me be clear: being brave is not being reckless, and it is also not false bravado with metaphorical chest-pounding. We all have fears, and it is not wrong to be afraid, especially when there is a significant real threat to our lives. In EMS we go to great lengths to train on, and ingrain, the importance of scene safety, but the job still has inherent dangers and risks. What we cannot do is allow fear to determine our decisions, and that is where bravery comes in.

If we look back at my example of the Kentucky patient at the beginning of this chapter, I had a legitimate fear and concern that if I pulled the endotracheal tube, I might not be able to put a new tube in its place. Failure to do so could possibly have been deadly to my patient and a terminal event for my career. I also knew that if I allowed my fear to make the decision for me and I failed to act, it could also be detrimental to my patient. I had to be brave for my patient's sake and lean on the confidence in my training and skills. Most importantly, I had to lean on God that He would guide my actions. Some might say that my bravery to change the tube was ego or stupidity and that I only got lucky. Each is certainly entitled to their opinion, but I know I faced my fears that day and allowed God to guide me and use me for the betterment of that patient.

As a leader there will be many occasions when we will face challenges and adversity. Our daily decisions can have a profound effect on the people in our organization and their personal lives. The operational and budgeting decisions we make directly affect our employees' ability to provide for their families. If we make the wrong decisions, or fail to take appropriate actions, they could lose that ability, thus increasing their challenges and their fears. If we care about the people we lead, that is one of the weights we carry as leaders. When we have people whom we are responsible for leading, our bravery can be contagious. When the organization faces a crisis, is responding to a disaster, or has suffered a loss, we must step forward and be the brave leader that faces the challenge head-on without fear. We should be role models for our organization, taking advantage of every opportunity to lead by example and set the tone for our people. Our willingness to face dangers or challenges can inspire our team to face their own fears and, in turn, be brave themselves.

Being Balanced

"To everything there is a season, A time for every purpose under heaven; A time to be born, and a time to die; …"

Ecclesiastes 3: 1-2 NKJV

In all areas of our lives, we face dichotomies that require us to be balanced. Veteran Seals and authors Jocko Willink and Leaf Babin speak extensively on this subject in their book "The Dichotomy of Leadership". Among other dichotomies, they express the importance of being "resolute but not overbearing", being "aggressive but not reckless", and being "disciplined but not rigid". They expound on the traits of a great leader and how to balance those with opposing traits. They are much better experts on this balance, so I will let you seek the in-depth explanation from their writings if you choose.

In this instance, the dichotomy is to be bold enough to speak our minds and advocate for a just cause, while being balanced enough to not become overbearing or opinionated. We must be brave enough when confronted with adversity to meet it head-on and not allow our fear to decide our actions for us. While balancing our actions of bravery, we must not allow our courage to cause us to be completely reckless.

Our lives are all about balance. A good quality or personality trait can become a bad trait if we slide too far to that end of the spectrum. If we get out of balance, what is typically viewed as a strength can quickly become a weakness. What should guide us to success may end up leading us to failure if not properly equalized. In our spiritual lives, if we begin to rely too much on our own abilities and understanding, we become overconfident. This distances us from God. This is a place I have been too many times in my past.

I don't know that you can necessarily rely too much on God, but if you think He is going to make everything easy and require no work on your part, you have definitely swung to the wrong end of the spectrum. God certainly could have brought down the walls of Jericho without Joshua and his army. However, He still required them to march around the walls once a day for six days, and seven times on the seventh day, before He brought down the walls. We need balance to be effective as Christians, spouses, parents, friends, professionals, and leaders. Having balance requires constant self-evaluation and awareness. If we are dedicated to finding that balance, we can be successful in fulfilling our God-given purpose.

As we can see, boldness and bravery will be required throughout our lives. While they have significant similarities, they also have distinct differences. When we are bold, we are willing to take calculated risks and speak up, and we will be known for our confidence. When we are brave, we show our courage and our God-given resolve to face any danger, and we embolden others to be brave also. We must remember to be balanced, lest our boldness become arrogance, and our bravery become reckless abandon. When we understand the necessity for both boldness and bravery, and have an intimate knowledge of their contrasts, we can be balanced and effective in any role God calls us to fill. I pray we each go forth with boldness and bravery, knowing that God will be with us each step of the way.

CHAPTER 7

Revealing His Vision

"For the vision is yet for an appointed time; But at the end it will speak, and it will not lie. Though it tarries, wait for it; Because it will surely come, it will not tarry." Habakkuk 2:3 NKJV

If you had asked me in my early years as a paramedic, "What do you want to be in five years?", I would have told you I wanted to be someone respected by my peers and be a paramedic preceptor who students wanted to ride with and learn from. Eventually, I wanted to become a flight paramedic. Being in a supervisory or leadership role was not on my radar, nor was it a goal I had set for myself. I did not view myself as a leader nor did I think I had the skills necessary to become the director of my service. We already had a director, and we certainly had several paramedics I looked up to, and I anticipated they would fill that role should it come open.

I am not sure why I did not have that long range vision for where God was leading me. Maybe it was my lack of self-confidence, maybe I was too caught up in the immediate day-to-day. Most likely it was because I was not focusing on staying in tune with God's voice and letting it guide me. After all, God had already laid some of the groundwork to guide me toward leadership. Throughout my life, He had used people to give me subtle hints and gentle nudges toward this role. The signs were all around me, even when I was a kid.

At my church we had a class on Wednesday nights for boys called Royal Ambassadors (RA), which was similar in some ways to Boy Scouts. We learned some survival skills and engaged in some activities, all while learning the Bible and how to become strong Christian men. Our leader for most of my years in that class was David Province, a strong man of faith with the most loving and friendly personality. All of us looked up to David and I must say that, outside of my father, he probably had the greatest impact on my Christian Walk and the man I am today.

David had a special way of connecting to, and encouraging, each of us. I remember very distinctly one night David was teaching us about spiritual gifts and how we should use them to honor God. He went around the room telling each of us the qualities he had seen in us, and he listed at least one God-given gift that we could use for God's divine purpose in our lives. When he got to me, he told me I was going to be a leader. Having low self-confidence, I thought he had it very wrong; there was no way God could use me to lead anyone or anything. I asked him why he thought I could be a leader. I asked what he saw in me that made him believe that was my gift. He told me I was always stepping up when we worked on projects, I was always willing to work, and I didn't care to get others involved in helping if they were standing around.

At the age of 16, my church family again saw something in me and, trying to nurture it, asked me to lead our "training union", which was our Sunday night bible study program. It was a small role that required me to give a brief bible devotion to everyone before they broke out in different age group classes. I reluctantly agreed, and that responsibility led me to study my bible and prepare like I never had before. It brought me closer to God and began to show me that he could use me, but at that point in my life I still didn't have any idea where it would go.

I had never really perceived the leadership qualities others were seeing in me but, looking back, I can see what David and others were talking about. That interaction with David, and what he shared with me, has always stuck with me. But the crazy thing is that I didn't put more value in it at the time, and I lacked his vision deep into my adult life.

Because of this lack of vision, I did not put much thought into preparing myself with leadership classes or leadership books. I wasted my early years in EMS not leading myself; I did not put any effort into preparing myself to fulfill the purpose God had for me and the vision he had laid out before me through that brief interaction with a Godly role model. Thankfully, the leaders in our EMS agency saw something in me and began taking actions that forced me to grow. Even though I was too naive to realize what they were doing at the time, God was still working.

Our deputy director, Charlie Williams, had the vision and the desire to develop young leaders. He knew that one day someone would need to take his place or the place of our director, Jack. He also had the foresight to know that, by developing leadership skills within the field level employees, ultimately that would make the agency better and make his job easier. He asked me to lead a quality improvement review team because, according to him, he had too much other work to do already. Looking back, I realize that God was using him to begin my leadership journey. I asked him if he was sure I was the right one and I threw out some names of several more experienced paramedics. He assured me he and Jack had discussed it in great detail, and they thought I was the right one to get this project going and cultivate it. I valued their confidence but was still unsure of myself. They allowed me to recruit several others to help with the review of patient care reports, and I developed a system of specifics to be analyzed and a process for how we would accomplish the work. Charlie and Jack agreed to the plan and allowed me to proceed. Little did I know the path this would propel me down.

Like many EMS leaders, when I was promoted, I felt I was given a titled role because I was good at being a paramedic and had built a decent reputation. Until that point, being a good preceptor to paramedic and EMT students was as far as I wanted to go into leadership because my personal desire was to be a flight paramedic. I had no desire to be an EMS supervisor, and I definitely did not see myself ever being the director of an EMS agency. God, as always, knew what He was doing, and He had a plan and purpose for me. I was a reluctant and wayward traveler on this journey, but God continued to light the path I should follow.

The thing that is so great about God's sovereignty is that He will not give up on you if you miss the message the first time around. If He has a purpose for you, and I promise He does, He will continue to point you in that direction no matter how reluctant, blind, or deaf spiritually you happen to be. There are many examples of reluctant leaders in the Bible. Moses said he couldn't speak well, and God put forth Aaron to speak for him, yet God used Moses to lead a whole nation out of captivity. Most are familiar with what happened when Jonah ran from God's command to preach in Ninevah. Jeremiah was appointed by God as a prophet but said he was too young. However, after God promised to always be with him, he went forth and fulfilled God's purpose. Peter, in a moment of fear and weakness, denied he was a follower of Christ even though he had journeyed with Jesus and witnessed his miracles. Peter still became a pillar of the early church.

Don't misunderstand, we can certainly drag our feet and disobey God's call long enough that we miss the opportunity. However, God will accomplish His will with or without us. I missed the signs God had placed in front of me many times in my life, mostly due to complacency in my spiritual life and a lack of aligning my vision with His vision. My RA leader, David, and my Deputy Director, Charlie, both saw something in me that I didn't see in myself. As I look back, there were several times in my life prior to EMS when I was placed in some type of leadership role. Most of the time I didn't realize it because it may not have been a titled role, but you don't always need a title to lead.

Charlie eventually left to become an instructor at our local community college. That created openings in the management team and, at the time, the policy of the local government was that any supervisor had to live in the county. I did not meet this criterion. Even though I grew up in Jefferson County and my family all still lived there, my wife and I had decided to live in the adjacent county to split the driving distances between our workplaces. That made me ineligible for any promotion, and at this point I didn't want one anyway. I was comfortable where I was.

Some of my talented colleagues were promoted into those roles and began to take on the quality improvement system I had worked to get up and running. I was cool with that, as it was less work for me that I wasn't getting anything extra for anyway. I still was not focused on where God was leading me, but He kept putting growth opportunities in front of me. I became an instructor in several continuing education courses to be a better preceptor, or so I told myself. In reality, it was another area in which God was growing me, teaching me to communicate, to learn even more about people and their personalities and how to motivate them. As it turned out, I was skilled at teaching. I enjoyed watching people learn new things and relished the excitement in their eyes when everything clicked.

At this stage, I had been a paramedic about 10 years and had established a good reputation for myself with my coworkers and my leadership. During that time, I had been allowed to help a couple of other instructors get our American Heart Association training center established. After it had been in operation for a few years, I was subsequently asked to lead it. Mind you, I was still on the truck working my regular 24-hour shifts and this was not an extra paid position. It was something a few of us did for the love of teaching and to help our fellow employees get better training. Once again, it was another leadership role God had placed me in to continue to propel me toward His purpose for me.

Soon thereafter, we received notice that our director, was being replaced by our deputy director, Jeff Coffey. I was sitting at my station one evening when Jeff stopped by. We had now known each other for years and worked on multiple calls and scenes together, so it was not unusual for him to stop by and chat. He asked if I could step outside to talk in private and I, of course, thought I was in trouble. I guess he could sense I was apprehensive and he told me it wasn't anything bad, he only had something to ask me.

Once we got outside, he proceeded to tell me he wanted me to be his deputy director of EMS. I told him I wasn't sure if I was the right one, but I appreciated the confidence he had in me so I would consider it. I reminded him that a glaring issue I saw was that I still did not live in the county. However, if he could get that policy changed, I would definitely pray about it and talk it over with my wife. He told me he didn't think the living requirement would be an issue if I stayed in the county during the nights I was expected to cover the on-call responsibilities.

I finished my shift that night with several prayers and contemplation, and the next day I talked with my wife. We spent some days in prayer, and both felt that God was pointing me in that direction. I called Jeff and told him I would do whatever he needed me to do as long as I didn't have to move from our home. He agreed and, shortly thereafter I was promoted to deputy director. I soon found it was a huge learning curve for me, as there was no succession guidance at this point and Jeff was busy learning his new role as well. We leaned on each other and grew together. We had no idea what the future held for either of us, but I still knew that God's plan was the right plan. I knew Jeff was a strong Christian also and I trusted he too was following God's direction.

I immersed myself in learning as much as I could about scheduling shifts, ordering supplies, managing people and personalities, managing budgets, and fostering relationships with other agencies. I wanted to be the person employees came to when they needed something, and I wanted to be the person Jeff came to when he needed something done. I became very task-oriented, which didn't leave a lot of room for self-growth. I made plenty of mistakes in those first couple of years in a supervisory role, but I was getting the hang of it.

It had been two years with Jeff as director and myself as his second when he came to me and told me he was feeling led to go back into law enforcement and become a state trooper. I was caught off guard and certainly never saw that coming. He told me his recommendation to the county mayor was going to be that I be his replacement. I told him I appreciated his support and his mentorship, and I would begin praying about it in case the mayor approached me. I explained it all to my wife that night and she began to pray as well.

Soon thereafter, Jeff turned in his resignation and the mayor asked me to take an interim role for the next few months until he could work through the process of officially replacing Jeff. I agreed to fill the interim position and do whatever was in the best interest of the agency. I was grateful for the opportunity, but even more thankful for the time gap, as it gave me much needed time to pray and contemplate what God really wanted me to do. I wanted to make sure that I was following God and not my own desires or the desires of another person.

In January 2005 I was named director, and a new stage began. I still had a lot to learn and many hurdles to clear. It helped that I was at a well-established agency with an awesome group of colleagues who knew their jobs and were great at taking care of people. I am not implying that we were perfect, and I was far from where I needed to be as a leader at this point. I knew God had walked me through this door despite my lack of vision and preparation. I also knew He had been secretly preparing me, and He had gifted me with certain abilities that would help me accomplish His purpose if I focused on Him.

As an individual, and as a leader, we must stay connected to God's purpose and we must see ourselves through His eyes. We must seek His guidance and His direction. If we fail to see the gifts He has given us, the passions He has instilled in us, and the path He has laid out for us, we will not be prepared for tasks He would have us do. I didn't see what others saw, that God had gifted me with the talents and qualities to be a leader. It stunted my growth as a Christian and as a leader, which inevitably led to me failing certain people I was meant to serve. In various situations, deep down I knew I was not fulfilling all the purposes for which I was created.

The great thing about God is that, despite our failures and lack of vision, He never gives up on us and He continues to forgive us. He continues to guide us back on track and propel us down His path to affirm His reason for creating us. We are all leading someone in some aspect of our lives, whether intentionally or simply by example. We should be following, and allowing ourselves to be led by, God. We need His prescience and focus to look inside ourselves for the gifts He has given us to share, and to find the purpose He has for each of us in this world. We must be able to see ourselves through the eyes of our colleagues, our mentors, and, most importantly, our Creator.

CHAPTER 8
Your Royal Court

"Listen to counsel and receive instruction, that you may be wise in your latter days" Proverbs 19:20 NKJV

We all have people who shape and influence our lives as we go through different stages and pass assorted milestones. Our parents, grandparents, teachers, pastors, coaches, bosses, co-workers, and our friends alternately serve in this role. It is extremely important to have good role models and mentors in all aspects of our lives. Often, when people reach a titled or established leadership position, many adopt the idea they have arrived and that they should have all the answers. They adopt the false assumption that, because they have achieved a certain leadership position, they are expected to know everything and should not need to seek advice or consult others regarding decisions.

Certainly, this is a dangerous philosophy to adopt, even more so for young or new leaders. Without a doubt, as a leader, people will come to you for answers to difficult questions or problems. For this reason, leaders need to have a broad vision for their organization, their people, and for themselves. As leaders, we need to see beyond today to visualize where our organization needs to go and how to propel our people in the right direction to reach that destination.

Really great leaders realize they don't have to have all the answers or ideas. These truly great leaders know they need talented people around them to help fill their gaps. I am no different and, while I would not classify myself as a "great leader", I have had a modicum of success and certainly could not have achieved that without an exceptional team around me.

My closest advisors and mentors are vitally important to the decisions I make and to the success of the organizations I have had the privilege to lead and serve. In my mind, I have always thought of this as my "royal court". Let me give one quick disclaimer: because I am using the royal court analogy does not mean I feel we should be rulers or dictators. We are placed in our leadership positions to serve God and, ultimately, to serve our people, not to lord over them.

Throughout history, in numerous cultures and societies, emperors and kings have had royal courts. They surrounded themselves with key people who brought special talents and areas of expertise to fulfill important roles. The members of the royal court were there to assist and advise the leader, to help them deal with the daily business of managing the kingdom and providing for their people. Even King Solomon, who was known as one of the wisest kings in the Bible, had a royal court to provide advice and counsel.

As leaders, we all need some version of a "royal court". First and foremost, like King Solomon, our initial counsel in any decision needs to be with God. It is from Him that all true knowledge and wisdom emanates. We also need informed and committed people around us to help advise us and counsel us when we face tough decisions.

You might ask why we need a "royal court". I have learned from experience that no matter how smart you may think you are, or how skilled you may be as a leader, at some point you are going to encounter a problem that you are not ready for or are not experienced enough to know how to handle. We all have our own faults, weaknesses, and blind spots. We need identifiable people with special skills, knowledge, and talents to fill the gaps where we fall short. As a leader, the success and longevity of our organizations, and the quality of life of our people, depend on us making wise and well-informed decisions every day. To do this, we must have far-reaching vision to anticipate potential long-term effects and grasp how these decisions may impact the future of those we serve.

As servant leaders, we need quality people around us in key roles to advise us, coach us, counsel us, fight for us and our principles, and tell us when we are about to screw up things. We can certainly have as large a court as we need and, as our organization grows, our court will naturally need to be bigger. Nonetheless, I have identified at least four key trusted individuals who I always make sure I have in my corner. In some cases, one person may fill multiple roles, or may fill different roles in different circumstances or parts of our lives. Regardless, we all need these key positions in our court: the coach, the critic, the counselor, and the champion.

The "Coach"

"Remember those who rule over you, who have spoken the word of God to you, whose faith follow, considering the outcome of their conduct." Hebrews 13:7 NKJV

When I was nine years old, I convinced my parents to sign me up for "minor league" baseball. My sister, who was 16 at the time, was already a talented first baseman on her softball team. I had spent numerous hours watching her and her team practice and play, thus inspiring me to be part of such a team playing a sport with which I had fallen in love.

I had seen my parents support and encourage her. I saw how they enjoyed watching her and the pride they had in her success. Therefore, I assumed when I asked if I could try out to be on a baseball team it would be no problem. However, my parents were a bit reluctant. They were concerned because I was much smaller than the other kids my age. They were afraid I would get hurt and would not be able to compete.

I continued my pleas for a chance to play. I began to practice on my own at home and outside the ball field while my sister practiced with her friends. I would be outside every chance I got, tossing a baseball in the air to catch fly balls or bouncing it off a nearby wall to field grounders. Anytime I could get someone to pass with me or pitch to me, it was even better. Finally, my persistence paid off and, with a little encouragement from my sister's softball coach, they agreed to let me try out for baseball.

My first glove was a hand-me-down from my sister. It was slightly big for me, but it was well broken in. I didn't care what glove I had as long as I got to play. Thankfully, after try-outs, I was chosen for a team. My first coach was Ronnie, a young man with no kids of his own on the team who simply had a passion for baseball and for helping us have a good time learning a sport. I am not sure why he picked me, and I am sure that even when he did, I was probably one of the last ones chosen given my lack of physical attributes. He didn't seem to care that I was small, and he devoted time to working with me and the entire team. He identified our strengths and our weaknesses, and taught us how to utilize them and hone them for the success of the team.

Ronnie identified that I had better-than-average speed and an instinct for judging and catching fly balls. I guess those countless hours of playing catch by myself, and with my friends at my sister's softball practices, paid off. Ronnie placed me in one of the outfield positions; we all knew the best kids our age played in the infield, but I didn't care. I was happy to get a chance to play.

It turns out I was good at those outfield positions. However, I was not so good at the plate. Being small, most of the bats our team had were too big and too heavy for me to swing fast enough to catch up to the pitches. I struggled in practice to make contact, even when my coach was pitching slow, easy tosses to help us learn. He worked with me extra after practice on several occasions, teaching me to choke-up on the bat and position my feet correctly. I could sense he wanted me to succeed, not only for the team, but for my own confidence and enjoyment of the game. I continued to improve a little each practice but, with my small size, even when I made contact the ball didn't go very far. I don't know if I ever got it out of the infield during practice. I think coach saw potential value in the fact I was a left-handed batter and I had a small strike zone, both qualities that gave pitchers problems, especially at our age.

The first game finally arrived and, to no surprise, when I walked in the dugout and looked at the lineup, I was at the bottom. At least I was in the lineup and not on the bench, although the coach didn't have much choice as there were only 10 of us on the team. I don't remember all the details of that first game except that I didn't get much action in right field and I struck out my first two times at the plate.

What I do remember is, as fate would have it, I came up to bat in the bottom half of the last inning; there were two outs, a runner on second base, and we were behind by one run. I could feel the tension of the whole situation building up inside me. I am pretty sure I could hear my teammates groan as I walked up. The first pitch was right down the middle, but I totally whiffed: strike one. Thanks to my small strike zone, the second and third pitches were high, for ball one and two. The fourth pitch was a beauty and I swung almost out of my shoes, but I hit nothing but air: strike two.

My coach called time and had me meet him on the third base line. I am sure he could see my lack of confidence and wanted to calm me down. He wanted to win this game, my teammates wanted to win this game, and this little runt of a kid with a two and two count was currently their only chance to continue the game. Ronnie kneeled and told me, "Kid, you still got a chance. You're a left-handed batter and you are fast. I don't need you to hit it to the outfield, I need you to get on base." He told me we had the top of the order coming up, and they could get us around if I got on base safely.

He whispered in my ear the plan. If it was a strike, I needed to hold my bat out and let the ball hit it and run like heck. If the pitch wasn't close to being a strike, I should try to take the walk. I walked back to the left-hand batter's box, still nervous and, likely, even shaking. The next pitch came, and it was high: ball three. I was hoping for the next pitch to be high as well, and I am sure my whole team, my parents, and my teammates' parents were hoping for ball four also.

The pitcher went into his wind-up and delivered a beautiful pitch right down the middle. I held out my bat and, truth be known, probably closed my eyes. Luckily the ball found my bat, barely, but it made enough contact for the ball to dribble slowly toward third base. I was in a state of shock for a split second and then I took off toward first base as fast as I could. The pitcher and third baseman both went after the ball that was barely staying fair as it rolled slowly along the base line. Would it stay fair or foul? I had no idea; I was running for my life.

My foot hit the bag, the throw was late, and the umpire signaled I was safe. In all the commotion, the runner at second had been able to make it to third, since the shortstop failed to cover it when the third baseman went for the ball. I was excited! What coach had told me had worked and, even more importantly, I hadn't failed my team. Our lead-off batter was next, and we now had a chance to win this game. The first pitch was belt high and right over the heart of the plate. He blasted a long fly toward center and I took off to second. As I rounded the bag, I heard the fans of the other team cheer, and the other team begin to celebrate. The centerfielder had made the catch, out number three, and the game was over.

All was not lost that day, and it was only the first game. I had gained some confidence in myself and in my coach. My coach also learned something about me. He learned I would listen to him; I would do what he asked me to do, and my speed could be a factor. I can't really remember how many games we won or lost that year. What I do remember is I became a bunt specialist and eventually even got to be at the top of the line-up a few times. My coach Ronnie left a lasting impression on me. He was one of the first who showed confidence in me, and for that I have always been grateful.

As I grew older, I had several other coaches, not only in sports, but in several areas of my life. I had spiritual coaches at my church who helped me grow closer to God and be a better Christian. There have been several different men who inspired me, led me, and coached me into becoming a man of integrity who strives to treat people right. They came from different parts of my life; some were farmers I worked for, others were professors at the college where my mom worked and I spent my summers hanging out, some were teachers who went beyond the classroom to see potential in me as a young man. In my EMS career I have always had mentors I not only looked up to, but I relied on to help guide me during the times when I wasn't sure of my direction, purpose, or abilities. These "coaches" in my life have been instrumental in helping me become the man that God would have me to be, and the paramedic and leader I was meant to be. They saw potential in me and nurtured my talents to help me fulfill my purpose.

As leaders we are also often placed in the role of "coach" for many of our team members, but we need coaching too. We should each continually be working to be the best we can be, which will undoubtedly require some coaching. None of us are perfect, nor do we always see the areas in which we can improve. That is where the coaching comes in, and that is why I always have "coaches" in my corner helping me identify my strengths, pointing out my weaknesses and blind spots, and helping me develop a game plan to maximize those strengths while overcoming the weaknesses.

A great coach is knowledgeable about their craft, they are honest with their players, and they want the best for those they are coaching. A great coach values the success of each person they coach, not only because they get satisfaction from your wins, but because they care about you as an individual. We all need great coaches in our corner no matter how many positions we move up or how many so-called championships we win. None of our success is strictly our own doing, and having great coaches in our "court" can only help us reach even greater success in fulfilling our purpose.

The "Critic"

"As iron sharpens iron, so a man sharpens the countenance of his friend." Proverbs 27:17 NKJV

The word critic comes from the Greek word kritikos, which means able to discern. Kritikos is, in turn, derived from the word krités, meaning a person who offers reasoned judgment or analysis. We see critics most often in such areas as fashion, food, film, literature, and art. They are usually experts in their field who others respect and whose assessments and judgment are valued. They often use industry standards and guidelines to objectively evaluate their subject and be fair in their assessment.

There is a distinct difference between being a critic and only being critical. Those who simply want to put forth their own position or opinion for their own recognition or personal gain should not be considered as a critic under the true definition. Take, as an example, a food critic who is invited to a new upscale restaurant by the owner to evaluate the food, service, and atmosphere. The owner invites respected critics hoping that a good review will add validity to their product and improve their business. They know they will get an honest, unbiased review and this will help them identify areas they can improve.

Compare that to a social media influencer or self-proclaimed critic who reviews that same restaurant. They may have a preconceived agenda, a previously established bias, or they may post whatever they think will get them the most interactions or "likes". This is not necessarily an honest evaluation. We have all seen the never-satisfied customer who loves the attention of posting negative comments online, all for the adulation and perceived power it appears to provide them. It is the motive of the individual that separates the critic from the purely critical. If the advice or opinion is fueled by self-serving motives, the individual is criticizing to harm or destroy. The true critic seeks to inform and advise, with an end goal to help people make wise decisions or improve processes.

Part of my job since 2009 has been as a tactical medic for our Sheriff's Department Special Operations Team. As part of my training for that role, I attended several different SWAT courses to learn special tactics in movement, weapons, teamwork, care under fire, and tactical medicine. The weapons and tactics part of that training was a huge learning curve for me because, as a street medic, we are usually on the perimeter in a safe place during high-risk calls. As a tactical medic, I would now technically be in the line of fire and operating as part of a team in a high-risk environment. We all know that any team is only as strong as its weakest link.

In those training sessions my instructors put us in high-stress scenarios and pushed us to our limits, all because they knew our lives depended on the quality of our training and the proper execution of what they were teaching us. At the beginning of the SWAT course, they would walk us through the scenarios and then gradually increase the difficulty and speed at which we needed to move. I struggled at the beginning, but by the end of the course we were all becoming smoothly oiled machines. Part of our training, despite what our anticipated role on our respective teams would be, was that we had to complete a final evolution as the team leader. Part of that final evolution was an evaluation of our performance during the entire course, as well as how we handled the role of team leader in the final scenario.

    My instructors sat down with me to critique my performance. They told me they were impressed with my poise and self-control, they felt I had gained a solid grasp of the tactical concepts, and they were pleasantly surprised with my competency with the weapons. As with any good critique, they also had to address the areas in which I needed improvement. And I had plenty to improve on; my instructors hammered me on the need to be more vocal in communication with my team, making sure I gave them direction and called out hazards or blind spots. I had taken a couple of unnecessary risks in an effort to move exceptionally fast but had gotten lucky in the final scenario. They also told me I needed to get physically stronger if I was going to be responsible for moving an injured officer in full gear by myself. It was valuable feedback, and it gave me goals to strive for after I completed the course. A knowledgeable and honest critic in any environment is extremely important and can possibly be lifesaving.

    It is the true critic we need in our court. We need them to always watch and evaluate our decisions, our plans, and our relationships. We need them to be honest, unbiased, and unselfish. They are important and necessary to hold us accountable and to keep us authentic. I have had plenty of people be critical of my decisions, and even my successes, but I tried not to pay attention to the detractors. As leaders there will be plenty of people who can be critical, but very few who can serve in our court as the critic.

Some of the people in my court I have valued the most have been my critics. They were the ones I knew would come to me if they saw me making a bad decision, responding to a situation inappropriately, or heading down the wrong path. They came to me out of love and a humble desire to see me succeed. I can't express enough the value of having a trustworthy critic in your court. They will keep you grounded, honest, and growing. Choose wisely.

The "Counselor"
"Where there is no counsel, the people fall; but in the multitude of counselors there is safety." Proverbs 11:14 NKJV

Throughout my life and career I have had many counselors. In making decisions we all need input and guidance from time to time, and I am certainly not smart enough to make all my decisions solely on my own. I seek the counsel of God first, through prayer and reading His Word. I also know it is important to have people in our lives to whom we can turn in times of difficulty to counsel us, help us work out the next steps, and help us find the correct path to take. I caution you that, when seeking counsel, you need to make sure you seek wise, Godly people.

My most trusted and consistent counsel in my life has been my wife. She is a Godly woman with a strong character and is grounded in her faith in Jesus. She is always honest with me, even when I may not want her to be. I know she loves me and she has always wanted the best for me. If I face a difficult life decision, after I pray about it, I go to Rhonda. She has steered me back on the right track several times when I have veered in the wrong direction. She is my confidante and she knows me better than anyone else. The amazing thing is that, even though she knows me so well, she has chosen to stay with me all these years.

In my professional career, including my time as a leader, I have had many different counselors at different times and for different circumstances. When faced with a situation I was not sure how to handle, I turned to someone I trusted, someone I knew had experience with the problem or subject that was vexing me. I sought people I knew would be honest with me and whose expertise and opinions I valued.

In my early years as a paramedic, one of my trusted counselors was my first paramedic partner, Don. As I previously stated in Chapter 5, I first started working with Don when I was a young EMT in Grainger County, Tennessee. He was patient with me, and always displayed confidence and calmness on our emergency calls. He began to mentor me and was one of the people who originally encouraged me as a still-inexperienced EMT to go to paramedic school. We spent countless hours together answering calls and hanging out at the station, and we became very close. He was someone I looked up to, and I modeled many of my behaviors and patient interactions after qualities I saw in him.

When I became a paramedic, I would often consult Don about difficult calls I had made, and I would seek his input on how he would have treated the patient. One particular call after which I sought his counsel involved a middle-aged male with trouble breathing. We had arrived at the patient's home to find a fiftyish-year-old man sitting in his living room complaining of sudden onset of shortness of breath. The patient informed us he was up that morning and taking a shower when he suddenly had some sharp pain in his chest and started struggling to breathe.

I performed my initial assessment and placed him on supplemental oxygen, then moved him to the stretcher and out to the ambulance. I was questioning him about his medical history as I finished securing him to the stretcher. The patient informed me he had suffered a broken femur following a fall about four weeks prior, and it had been surgically repaired. He stated everything had seemed to be fine post-surgery other than some pain and soreness. He did state that the night before he had radiating pain in his hip and lower back. I noted it in my mind but, with my preconceived notion that this man may be having a myocardial infarction, I had failed to link the recent fracture to the current complaint.

We loaded the patient in the back of the ambulance and, before my partner closed the doors, the man's wife told him she loved him and asked me to take good care of him. She said she would meet us at the hospital. I told her I would take good care of him and would see her shortly. The patient requested the hospital where he had been treated before, which was about a 35-minute transport, so I told my partner I would finish starting the IV and administering any medications enroute.

I continued my assessment and placed my patient in a position of comfort to help him breathe easier. His oxygen saturation was a little lower than normal but nothing drastic. I continued supplemental oxygen at a modest rate and his oxygen saturation improved slightly, his chest pain resolved, and all his vital signs and ECG were normal. I started an IV and the patient began to complain about nausea, so I administered some medication to help him feel more comfortable. I worked through the rest of my respiratory distress and chest pain protocol and he seemed to be responding well, or so I thought.

As we were exiting the interstate to turn onto the street where the hospital was located, my patient suddenly became diaphoretic and said he thought he was going to vomit. I grabbed the emesis bag I had laid out and sat him fully upright to assist him if he indeed did vomit. As I locked the head of the stretcher in the upright position, my patient suddenly became unconscious and unresponsive. I immediately repositioned him to see what was going on and I noticed he now had a change on the heart monitor to a very slow, wide complex rhythm. I checked for a pulse but there was not one palpable.

I realized immediately that my patient probably had just suffered a pulmonary embolus (PE). I yelled at my partner that our patient was now in cardiac arrest and to step it up, and he informed me that we were pulling into the hospital parking lot. I began chest compressions and, after backing into the ambulance bay, my partner went in to get a nurse to assist us since our patient status had changed after I had given the radio report. We rolled into the ER and assisted the nurses and the physician in their attempt to resuscitate our patient. We worked as hard as we could for at least an hour, but the doctor finally called it and determined the patient had indeed suffered a PE and there was no chance of survival.

Pulmonary embolus is a known complication following broken long bones and surgery. I knew this but failed to even consider it on this call until it was too late. I had developed tunnel vision related to chest pain and had focused on the strong possibility this was a cardiac event. Even if I had known, I would not necessarily have changed my treatment because we did not have any medication on the ambulance to prevent or stop the PE. I could have possibly positioned my patient differently, or I could have upgraded the mode of transport and gotten him to the hospital a few minutes faster. In all reality, the outcome was most likely going to be the same for this patient, as the embolus was well on its way to doing its damage before he ever called us.

Knowing this still did not help how I felt about losing this patient and it did not get any better as I was walking back out to the ambulance. As I exited the ER, I ran face-to-face into his wife, as she had just arrived and had no clue what had happened. When we last spoke, her husband was awake and seemed stable, and I had promised her I would take good care of him. She asked me how her husband did on the way down and where she could go to see him. I pulled her to the side and began to explain what had taken place as we arrived at the hospital, and that the doctor would want to meet with her to explain further. I looked her in the eyes and told her how sorry I was and that I never expected things to take this devastating turn. I made sure the nurse and doctor were ready to meet with her and I walked her back to her husband's room. To say the least, she was devastated. I too was devastated, and I felt defeated. I had made a promise that I was not able to keep, so why would she, or anyone, ever trust me again.

    We cleaned our truck and started back to the county. I spent the whole ride second-guessing myself and analyzing every minute of that call. I turned it all over in my mind, every action I had taken or possibly failed to take. My EMT partner was asking me questions about what we could have done better, but I currently did not have those answers. When we got back to the county, I found a way to meet up with Don. I wanted to know what he would have done differently and if he would have recognized the root of the problem sooner.

    He knew exactly what was wrong with my patient within the first two sentences of my description. He asked me pertinent questions and proceeded to reassure me that what I had done or not done would not have changed this patient's outcome. Even if we had gotten him to the ER 10 minutes sooner, they would not have had time to stop the embolus; the patient would have still gone into cardiac arrest.

Don had been where I was, he understood what I was feeling, and he counseled me on how to deal with the loss and feelings of defeat. He reminded me of the importance of being open-minded and avoiding tunnel vision on my calls. He was fair and honest with me because he wanted to see me grow and continue to be successful. That is the very definition of a counselor in action. I was blessed to have Don as a mentor and a counselor during my career.

There have been many times during my career as a leader that people have come to me and asked for my opinion or advice. They have sought my counsel on a vast array of EMS calls, personal issues, career decisions, and simply the everyday struggles of life. Most times I wondered why they would come to me, as I do not possess any great wisdom. Maybe it is my established title, but I hope it is because they know I have walked a similar path and that I care about them as individuals. The truth is, most people already have access to the answers they seek if they are in constant counsel with God and they listen to that still small voice inside them. We need to be willing to be a counselor to our people when they need us. But, as a leader, there will be times when you will need not only the counsel of God but the wise counselor in your court.

The "Champion"

"Arise, O Lord, in your anger; lift Yourself because of the rage of my enemies; Rise up for me to the judgement you have commanded!"   Psalm 7:6 NKJV

We often read about the use of champions in warfare in writings from ancient history, epic poetry, mythology, and, of course, the Bible. Armies on the battlefield would send forth their best warriors, a champion or sometimes multiple champions, from each side to battle one another. Their fight would decide the winner and spare the death of hundreds, if not thousands, of their soldiers. The most common reference we read about in the Bible is that of the battle between the Philistines and the tribes of Israel.

As it is described in 1 Samuel, the armies of Israel and the Philistines were encamped on either side of a valley. Every morning and every evening, the champion of the Philistines, Goliath, would come out and taunt the Israelites, defying their God and daring them to send forth their best to fight him. All the battle-hardened soldiers of Israel were afraid of Goliath. Not only did he stand in at a domineering 9 feet 9 inches tall, but he was known as a fierce warrior. While none of the men in the army would go out to face him, a small shepherd boy was there one day delivering food to his brothers when he heard the champion's taunts. This young boy, David, approached the king and volunteered to face the Philistine champion.

Despite discouragement, David still pressed to proceed into battle. They attempted to give him armor but it was too big and heavy, and he elected to face the giant with his shepherd's sling and five smooth stones. He told his fellow Israelites that he did not rely on the armor, but instead he relied on God to protect him and defeat the giant. The arrogant giant mocked David and his small stature, and he mocked the God David believed in. David struck down Goliath with one stone thrown from his sling, knocking him unconscious and thus enabling David to cut off Goliath's head with the giant's own sword. Witnessing this, the entire Philistine army chose to flee.

There are other examples of champion warfare in the Bible and in literature. In Homer's *Iliad*, we read of the epic battle between Achilles and Hector. We see examples in Roman writings and their stories of the gladiators. These champions were sent forth to represent and defend their leaders, to stand for their honor, and to conquer their enemies, thus advancing the leader's objectives. **The phrase "champion a cause" comes from these stories; it means to fight for, defend, protect, maintain, or support a particular initiative.**

In our organizations and in our lives, there will be times when our principles and beliefs will be challenged. At times those challenges will come when we are not present to defend those values ourselves. This is where we need our champion, or champions, to stand up for our principles and beliefs in our absence, or to come along beside us when we are faced with these challenges. We need people of strong character who share our core principles. We need individuals who have bought into our vision and the direction in which we are steering our organization. That person is like David, not afraid because of their strong faith, and with a willingness to enter the arena and engage in battle. Of course, when I speak of battle, I speak metaphorically of a battle of ideals and beliefs.

One of the common themes in being the executive leader of a local government organization is that, even though you may not be a politician, you will have to deal with politics. If there ever was an arena ripe for battle, it is the political arena. There have been many challenges to me from various elected officials who oversee the budget allocations that my department receives. During a particular few years, after several changes took place in our local government, my leadership and the operation of our department was under extreme scrutiny. With the aid of a few of my own disgruntled employees, whose selfish motives led them to provide inaccurate and incomplete information to some elected officials, the new politicians were attempting to make me appear incompetent as a leader. I stood my ground during these ambushes at public meetings, and I was always able to counter with verifiable statistics and information to disprove their false allegations.

What I found out later was there were many champions fighting on my behalf behind the scenes. I had members of the community who had used our services, some of whom had brought me complaints that I had addressed, who were calling my attackers to vouch for my character and professionalism. I also had several loyal employees who leveraged their influence with the politicians, and who also sought out the dissenters within our ranks and called them out on the misinformation they were spreading. I had champions I did not even know about who entered the arena to fight on my behalf. If nothing else speaks to the outcome, the fact I have remained the director for over 20 years, longer than any director in the history of our organization, proves the value of having strong champions in your court.

If you are in leadership long enough, you will face challenges to your vision and standards. Some of those challenges will come to you straight on and you can choose to face those alone. However, I can attest that it certainly helps to have battle-hardened warriors standing beside you. The true value of your champion is displayed when you are not present and those challenges surface. The faithful champion will not hesitate to enter the arena and defend your position and do battle on your behalf. They will not sit idly by while someone mocks you or tries to discredit you and your position. The champion will dispel lies and rumors about you or your decisions.

With worthy and faithful champions in your court, your detractors will know you do not stand alone, and they will often choose not to challenge your position. While I prefer not to fight, and I try to seek common ground to reach resolution in disagreements, there are times when a battle needs to be fought. There will be times when we must not compromise our beliefs, our principles, and what we see as the right thing to do. At those times, we must make a stand. I reiterate that we are stronger when we do not stand alone, and we are well-served to have champions as part of our court.

While you may not choose to call it your "Royal Court" because it is a bit too goofy to you, the fact remains the same: we all have an "inner circle "and we need people in our court to give advice and counsel us in all aspects of our life. Our coaches help us identify and maximize our strengths, and they help us improve our weaknesses. A critic will honestly evaluate our decisions and our actions and provide an unbiased assessment to us when necessary. We need Godly people from whom we can seek counsel when we need guidance, or simply someone to whom we can vent our frustrations. And finally, in the times we are challenged in battle, we need our champions to enter the arena with us and help us defend our principles and beliefs. All leaders should have a strong group of talented, experienced, and trustworthy individuals in our court. They make us better leaders and servants to our people and, ultimately, the "kingdom" will be better for it.

CHAPTER 9
Firm, Fair, Flexible, Forgiving

"Masters, give your bondservants what is just and fair, knowing that you also have a Master in heaven." Colossians 4:1 NKJV

      We are all leading someone, even if we do not always realize it. And this leadership does not always require, nor does it always come with, a title. There are people watching what we do, what we say, and how we respond in life's various situations. Those of us blessed to be parents know that our little ones are always watching what we do. They have a natural tendency to look up to us; to want to do the things they see mom and dad doing. They will mimic what we say even if it's bad. They pick up on parts of our personalities and we see ourselves come out in them at different times. They will respond with similar emotions when they see those emotions displayed by us in times of excitement, joy, stress, and sorrow. We must be cognizant as parents that there are always little eyes watching us and little ears listening to us. If anyone in our lives really knows who we truly are, it is our kids. They see what we do and what we say, and these are the things that reflect our values and our character.

If you desire to be placed in a recognized leadership role, or you are already in a titled role as a leader, it is understood that there will be people who report to you. We are responsible as leaders to have a vision for the organization, but to also see areas of opportunity and growth for our people. Throughout my years in an executive leadership role, I have sought to base my decisions on what is best for the people who have been placed in my charge. What is best for my team as individuals will ultimately be what is best for the entire organization. Team members who have the tools they need to do their jobs efficiently and effectively will be more productive. If they know that their leadership cares about them as individuals, they will be happier and, therefore, more loyal and eager to follow the vision and mission of the organization. I am not sharing any new or profound knowledge here. There are numerous books and podcasts on servant-style leadership. This is the style I have tried to model and utilize throughout my career.

Serving those we are tasked to lead is not always easy. Between different personalities, backgrounds, ethics, and family dynamics, leadership is challenging at best. One of the more difficult parts of leadership is holding our team members accountable. There will be times of conflicts, complaints, and sometimes sheer laziness. As a leader you will be called on to intervene in these situations. If you fail to do so, the individual will fail, the team will fail, and, if allowed to go unchecked, the organization could fail. I can tell you after 20 years as an executive leader; despite having an outstanding team, I have had to settle plenty of conflicts, address numerous complaints, motivate the low performers, and take corrective actions. I have not always handled them in the right way, but I have discovered four guiding principles I utilize in my leadership role to help me make the best decisions when dealing with my team. Those four principles are to be firm, fair, flexible, and forgiving.

Being Firm

Let me describe what I mean by being firm. As a leader I must always be firm in my beliefs, my ethics, and my standards. It is often stated that people will know what you believe not by the words you speak, but by the actions you take. Our actions point directly to our motives and beliefs, and I promise you that, similarly to our children, those we lead are watching what we do. We should never take the approach of "do as I say and not as I do". That means accountability starts with us, and every day we must endeavor to be firm in our standards. I have made mistakes, I have gotten lazy, but I have held myself accountable and acknowledged the times when I have messed up.

As a leader I know my team members are not perfect and they are going to make mistakes from time to time. I know I will have to hold them accountable when they go against the ideals and principles of the organization. I must be firm in holding everyone to the core values and principles of the organization and help everyone strive to reach their full potential. We all have times when we get a little lazy, lose our focus, are not aligned with the vision of the organization, or even blinded by our own success. We must firmly maintain our focus on the overall mission and how to keep pushing toward those goals. Renowned author and leadership expert Simon Sinek, in his book *Start with Why*, refers to this loss of focus as our "'why' becoming fuzzy". There will be times when we must remind ourselves and our team of why we are doing what we do so that our vision and mission are clear, and our objectives are achieved. To clarify, being firm does not mean being harsh or abusive. If we lose our temper or cross the line with an employee, we must be consistent in acknowledging our error and make a quick and immediate apology. Being firm means being steadfast in our values and principles regarding what is right and ethical in every situation and holding ourselves and our people to those standards.

Being Fair

When I was a kid and things did not go my way, I often responded with, "That's not fair". My parents would usually tell me, "Life's not fair". I found myself repeating that phrase to my son Joe. I don't know why I used that phrase with him other than it is what I had been told by my parents, and I had also learned it to be true as I grew older. It is also a lesson we see played out every day for those of us who work in EMS. It is also a lesson my son learned at much too young an age.

If anyone is aware that life is not fair, it is Joe. At three months of age, Joe contracted Respiratory Syncytial Virus (RSV). He continued to worsen and we took him to the doctor, who decided Joe needed to be admitted to our local hospital. He had been in the hospital a couple of days and my wife and I had taken off work and had been staying with him.

Joe had not really improved much, but still the doctor came in and told us he would be sending him home the next day.

The following day was my regular shift on the ambulance, and I didn't have much sick time, so my wife and I thought it would be okay for me to go back to work since they were sending Joe home that day. I went to work and, only a few hours into my shift, my wife called and I could hear the fear in her voice. She told me something had happened, and Joe had turned blue and stopped breathing for a few seconds. Luckily, they had not released Joe yet, and my wife said the nurses were in a panic and they were going to send Joe to a larger hospital. I immediately informed my boss that I needed to leave work and took off to the hospital.

When I arrived, they had Joe on a higher concentration of oxygen than before. He was no longer cyanotic, but I could tell he was getting tired and using more of his accessory muscles to breathe. I discussed with my wife that I would get one of our ambulances to transport him to the larger hospital and that I would ride with him. This was one of the perks of being a paramedic that I wish I had never had to use.

Once at the University of Tennessee Medical Center, we were initially admitted to the pediatric inpatient floor. It was a long first night, as Joe's oxygen levels kept getting lower, his breathing more labored, and he was not able to feed. Because of his struggles, the next morning Joe was placed in the neonatal intensive care unit (NICU). Due to its design at the time, and the severity of the patients in that unit, we were not allowed to stay with him 24/7. We set up camp with our family in the cubicle waiting area set aside for parents with children in the NICU, and we took turns seeing him every two hours during visitation times.

My wife and I entered the unit on one of those visits and walked in to see our tiny boy intubated and on a ventilator. We were shocked and furious. What had happened? Why didn't someone come talk to us? The nurses could tell by our faces that we had not been informed and began to apologize. They immediately called the pulmonologist to come meet with us. As a paramedic, I knew this wasn't good. But even my wife, with no medical training, knew this was an ominous sign.

Dr. McCarthy, the pulmonologist, met with us and explained that Joe was not progressing as he should; that his body was becoming too tired, so he needed the breathing tube and ventilator to allow him to heal and recover. As parents you never want to see your tiny baby clinging to life by a thread. We had several sleepless nights and prayed, probably like we had never prayed before. Dr. McCarthy told us he wanted to run some tests and that he thought there was a chance that Joe had a genetic disorder called Cystic Fibrosis (CF). As a paramedic I knew what it was, but I did not know much about it. My wife and I would soon learn much more than we ever wanted to about this rare but severe disorder.

The tests indeed confirmed that Joe had CF and thus his life, and ours, was forever changed. It meant numerous medications to help with digestion and nutrient absorption, breathing treatments to keep his airways open and thin the mucus, and chest percussion for 45 minutes twice daily to dislodge the mucus and clear it from his airways. All of this would be necessary for the rest of his life. We were told by Dr. McCarthy that our son's health, and his ability to live a productive life, was solely in our hands. If we were dedicated to doing what was required and aggressive in our treatment, our son could live into adulthood. If we were lazy and did not do his treatments and chest PT, Joe would spend countless days in the hospital and probably not live past the age of 20. I am forever grateful God placed Dr. McCarthy in our path at that point in our lives.

Joe spent hours each day doing treatments and chest PT, and we made sure he never missed the required therapy and he always took his medications. He grew up with all this being part of his daily routine and rarely did he question why. The doctor told us to let him be as normal as possible and not to shelter him. We were told Joe could have a great life if we allowed him to be active, exercise, and play like other kids. So that's what we did. We tried not to treat him any differently and, if you ask, he will say we probably pushed him more than most parents push their healthy kids. Despite our aggressive treatment regimen and everything we did each day to keep him healthy, he still had numerous hospital admissions and required home IV antibiotic therapy many times. There were holidays and birthdays spent in hospital rooms and, at times, he was very sick. That's the cruelty of CF.

Joe took it all in stride and, to this day, he is still one of the toughest kids I have ever known. He, like his mom and

I, loves sports and was always playing some kind of ball. Baseball and basketball were his favorites, and I enjoyed coaching his teams as he grew older. He was small for his age, but he was a talented athlete and worked hard to compete despite all the CF interventions he dealt with daily. Rhonda and I wanted him to enjoy life to its fullest, as we had almost lost him and we didn't know how long we would have him. Most importantly, we wanted him to see God in us and have his own personal relationship with Him. We also knew that God had given him to us for a reason. God had trusted us with the responsibility to teach him about Christ and keep him healthy because we knew God had a purpose for Joe.

Joe learned through his health struggles that life is not fair. I didn't need to tell him that because he was living it every day. The funny thing is when he, Rhonda, or I, started to think life was too unfair and wonder why Joe must go through so much, all we had to do was take a walk down any one of the hospital hallways and we could always find someone who had it way worse than us. We are thankful God gave Joe to us, and I wouldn't trade one moment. Joe is a grown man now. He is married and living a fulfilled life, approaching 30 years old at the time I am writing this. He has worked hard and still follows his treatment plan. Several years ago, he obtained a bachelor's degree in nursing and has been working as an ER nurse. He knows better than anyone that life is not fair, but he chooses not to fixate on what he didn't have. Instead, he focuses on how God has blessed him and how he can now help others.

As leaders we are expected to be fair and balanced in our decisions. We must first ensure that our decisions are not based on selfish ambition or personal gain, then we must also ensure that those decisions do not directly single out or discriminate against any group or individual. Also, when holding employees accountable to our policies and standards, we must be fair and equitable in our administration of those policies. However, we work in a world where "life is not fair", so no matter how hard we try, some things are going to be beyond our control.

There have been times I was accused as a leader of being unfair. When I was accused of unfairness, what I really wanted to say was what my parents had said, and what I had said to my son: "Life isn't fair". As a leader, we should fight the urge to take the easy way out and say that. Most often when we are accused of being unfair, it is because of a decision we made or a situation over which we have a modicum of control. We must at least consider that there is the possibility we have been unfair. Self-evaluation before we make decisions is key in trying to avoid unfairness but, once accused, we should reevaluate and look at it from the accuser's perspective as well.

It is easy to think that our decisions as leaders are always right, but I know for me that is not always true. If I am perceived as being unfair, I must first set my pride aside and seek to find out why, and from where, this sense of unfairness comes. There are times I made decisions I later realized were indeed unfair, and I did my best to right the wrong in those instances. There have also been times I made decisions that were perceived as unfair simply because whoever felt they had been wronged did not have all the details I did when making my decision. I have given unpaid leave after counseling and coaching an employee who was chronically late and abused their time, only to have them later make accusations that I was unfair because another employee who was late multiple times in a two-week period did not get days off. What the first employee did not realize is I had been informed by the second employee several weeks prior that their mother was battling cancer and was no longer able to babysit their child. This life change was going to cause the second employee to be about 30 minutes late on occasion for the next month until they could make other childcare arrangements. From an outside perspective, I was inconsistent in my disciplinary actions. Knowing all the details of the second employee, I was empathetic in my decision to allow them to briefly "bend" the rules for a short time because they notified me beforehand of their extenuating circumstances. Was I fair in my assessment and the decisions I made? I will let you decide. What I do know is that if the first employee had been in a similar situation to the second, they would have wanted me to allow them the same grace, and I would have given it. To me that is where the fairness of leadership meets the road.

There have been times in my life where I have accused God of being unfair, especially in relation to my son and all he has gone through. However, I always fall back to Isaiah 55:8-9 which reads, "My thoughts are nothing like your thoughts, says the Lord. And my ways are far beyond anything you could imagine. For as the heavens are higher than the earth, so my ways are higher than your ways and my thoughts than your thoughts." God can see far beyond what I can see, so I must trust that, when things don't seem fair, he knows all the details and ultimately his decision is what is best for me. As leaders we must follow God's example; we must look at all the circumstances of a situation, consider how a decision will affect the future of those involved, and make the best choice for the common good. Is that always going to be perceived as being fair? Obviously not. However, we must endeavor to be as fair and as equitable as we can in every situation and in every decision we make. That is our God-given duty and responsibility as a leader.

Being Flexible

I am a creature of habit and like to plan my days and weeks ahead of time. I like to clearly know what needs to be done and where I need to be. I work best with structure and direction, and that is part of who I am. My workdays typically start with some time for myself, which includes a quick strength workout at the gym before going into the office or to whatever commitment is first on my list for the day. After my workout, I get cleaned up and head in to get started on whatever tasks I have on my list to complete that day.

Most days I start with at least five things that need to get done before the day ends. However, working in any executive leadership role, and especially a leadership role in Emergency Management and EMS, my day rarely goes as planned. I have often joked that I come to work with five things on my list and often go home at the end of the day with those five things still on the list, plus five more. It has gotten a little easier over the years as my management team has grown and I have been able to delegate more, and I must say I am not sure how I did it many years ago without them.

It never fails, when you are the leader of an emergency service in a small county, that your day will be interrupted and hijacked with incidents and problems you need to respond to immediately. Managing and leading an EMS agency, there are always issues with equipment repairs, computer malfunctions, complaints, or any number of crises that will totally wreck your best laid plans for the day. Because of this, I had to learn to be more flexible in my desire to complete my list each day. There have been days I was on my way to the gym but had to divert straight to a scene call where tragedy had struck. There have been days when I had no sooner gotten home and sat down in the recliner than I had to get right back up and go in on a SWAT call. These instances have forced me to be more flexible and take things as they come each day.

As leaders we must also be flexible in our decision making. We don't have to have all the answers, and we certainly are not always right. We should be flexible enough to be open-minded when an employee or member of our management team comes to us with a different approach to a process or a new way to accomplish one of our routine operations. Because that is the way we have always done something does not always mean that it is the best way to continue to do it. I know I have been guilty of taking too much ownership in my policies or ideas. Primarily that is because I have often spent valuable time and effort in reaching my decisions, which naturally makes me think they are great ideas and causes me to plant my feet firmly on the subject.

I become so invested in some of my decisions that I become entrenched and inflexible. I have even, at times, been unapproachable by anyone with a different idea or way of doing something. Over the years I have learned more and more that I don't have to have all the ideas or be the smartest person in the room. I have learned to surround myself with intelligent people with special skills, and then create an environment that encourages them to come up with ideas and feel comfortable and free to share those with me. That is where the success of the organization multiplies and from where my success as a leader derives. These successes are not from anything I have done, but what the people around me have done. Being flexible regarding who makes decisions, and being open to new ideas, has been invaluable in many situations to me.

The one place as a leader that we cannot be flexible is in our character. We must have integrity in our leadership. We must follow through with what we say and what we promise to our people. We must take ownership when we fail to meet those pledges and expectations. If you have been in leadership for any length of time, your reputation will precede you when new employees talk with long-standing employees. When you interact with leaders in other organizations, what you say and do will influence them and reveal your character. If there is any flex in your core values, and any hint that you are not genuine or are "two-faced", you will not have long-term success, and you probably won't have many friends either. We should model that integrity to our employees and expect the same from them.

Over the years in my leadership journey, learning to be flexible has been one of my most valuable lessons. I must be flexible in my scheduling, my task list, and my decision processes. That flexibility has reduced my stress in some areas of my life and, at times, reduced some of the burdens of leadership. I think it has also made me more approachable and willing to listen to others' ideas and viewpoints. Being flexible in some areas helped reveal to me even more so how important it is to not be flexible in my integrity, as all relationships and successes hinge on those core parts of who we are. As leaders we must be firm and flexible at the same time.

Being Forgiving

If you are a Christian, you should certainly understand the concept of forgiveness. That is the whole purpose of why Jesus left the splendor of Heaven to die on the cross for our sins. He spoke and taught about forgiveness on many occasions, and He even included it when teaching us how we should pray. As the Lord's Prayer states, as recorded in Mathew 6:12 NKJV, "And forgive us our debts, as we forgive our debtors." In our spiritual life, we owe a sin debt to our righteous God. It is in our nature, it is a debt required to be paid with sacrifice, and it is a debt we could never pay on our own. If we expect God to forgive our trespasses, we must also be forgiving of those who trespass against us.

One of the things about becoming a supervisor or director in an organization where you have worked your way up through the ranks is that you will now be tasked with leading the people you were once working alongside, sometimes literally the day before. In my case I had been partners with many of the paramedics I was now expected to lead. We had run calls together, witnessed tragedies together, and shared meals, birthdays, and holidays together. They knew my strengths, but they also knew my faults and imperfections. Many of those paramedics had much more experience than I did at the time, and some of them were my mentors as I was entering EMS and learning the craft of being a paramedic. I had been promoted ahead of some of those who deserved the chance as much, if not more so, than I did. That dynamic is a difficult one to navigate, especially for a young leader with little experience or training in formal leadership.

In those first couple of years, I was trying to wrap my head around all the new responsibilities and pressures of leading my team. I did not always respond appropriately. I distinctly recall an incident with one of my team members in the early years of my role as director. Our service was undergoing some significant growth in personnel and call volume, and I had secured funding for new shifts and assignments. Now there were additional staff to manage, new personalities to learn, and changes to response plans and assignments. As we all know, change is not always easy and is not always received well, even when it makes your job simpler.

I caught wind that there were grumblings and dissatisfaction with some of the decisions I had made, and that several of the employees were questioning if I was the right one for the job. I was aware that a couple of the paramedics who were once my colleagues were trying to garner support for their preferences regarding how things should be done, and some felt they would be a better fit for my position. Maybe they thought I wouldn't find out, maybe they didn't care. I knew there was the possibility I had made some wrong decisions, or that I didn't communicate clearly to the staff the reason and purpose for those decisions.

This frustrated me and angered me at first. I felt it was an attack. I felt betrayed by some of the very people I worked side-by-side with, and some of whom I had even helped during a personal time of need. My default aggressive-defensive emotions were in full swing. I didn't like the attacks, and I was hurt by people I thought were my friends. Why didn't they come to me with their complaints? Did they think I was unapproachable? They certainly didn't care to come to me when they needed something in a time of crisis, so why would they think they couldn't come to me with a concern?

Initially I wanted to return the attack by going on the offensive. I had the power and authority to make changes that could certainly make their work harder and less pleasant, but that small voice inside was telling me that was not the right approach. I strongly considered leaving. If some of my employees wanted to replace me that badly, they could have it. I spent time in prayer and sought counsel from some close colleagues outside my agency. I kept coming back to the fact that God had placed me on this path and opened this door for me to be the director, and I needed to follow Him. He had placed me in this position, and He would remove me when it was His time. I needed to take ownership of any mistakes I might have made and work to resolve the issues.

I knew if I was going to stay, I needed to address this dissatisfaction head on. I began to individually meet with each employee, giving them the opportunity to give me their feedback, criticisms, and input. I even gave them an avenue to put those thoughts and grievances in writing anonymously and leave them for me to review. I got some valuable feedback from many of the employees, and I was able to see things from their perspective and, in some cases, explain mine. The ironic thing is some of the very ones who were secretly criticizing every decision I made sat in those one-on-one meetings and told me they supported me, and they didn't see why anyone would want my job. The anonymous written feedback revealed some additional areas in which I could improve my communication and bolster job satisfaction, but nothing balanced out the criticism that had been circulating from some of my detractors. At least now I had some areas I could address. Everyone knew I was open to listening to their concerns and the disparagers knew I was aware of what was happening.

I would still occasionally catch myself harboring some anger and frustration with those I knew were secretly trying to undermine my position. At times I allowed that frustration to boil to the surface, and I would lose my temper with them when they made a mistake or when I confronted them with untruths they had spread. I did not respond as a leader should, and I certainly did not respond as a Christian should. I had to, on many occasions, go back to those people and apologize for how I had responded and ask for their forgiveness. More importantly, to deal with the hurt and frustration I was feeling, I had to learn to forgive them as well.

There are always certain consequences to our actions, and giving or receiving forgiveness does not take away those consequences. Forgiving does not necessarily mean forgetting either. We simply can't wipe away hurt or mistreatment from our memory, as the human brain doesn't work that way. And while we have the capacity to forgive others, and most often should do so, we can still remember the trespass in order to protect ourselves from further harm. Forgiveness is often continual; it is a process and, for me, that process has often proven to be lengthy.

I had to try to follow the example of Joseph, one of the 12 sons of Jacob. In an example of ultimate betrayal, he was sold into slavery by his brothers. God had a purpose for it all and, after many years, Joseph rose to prominence in Egypt. Eventually his brothers had to come to him in a desperate time of famine. Joseph could have turned them away or even had them killed, yet he chose to forgive his brothers and thereby save his family and the entire 12 tribes of Israel. I had to find a way to forgive those who were attacking me and trust that God was in control and that I might be able to display the likeness and love of Christ during this storm. Eventually, not only was my character displayed, but my critics' true character was revealed.

"To whom much is given, from him much will be required," from Luke 12:48 NKJV, reminds us as leaders that our authority is ultimately given to us by God, and we have the responsibility to treat those we are placed in charge of serving as we would have God treat us. That is displayed in many ways, but most notably in our ability to grant forgiveness. I have hurt and offended others many times in my life, and I have sought forgiveness from those I realized I may have harmed. I have also tried to display and grant forgiveness to those who have wronged me, even when they did not seek my forgiveness. It has not been easy, but I am certain it has not been easy for others to forgive me either. It is a principle given to us by God. It is exhibited by Christ's death on the cross for our sins, and His resurrection that defeated death and gives us the path to eternal life. This was the ultimate display of forgiveness that none of us deserved, and the example of love for others we each should follow.

Whether it is the little all-seeing eyes of our children or the daily interactions with those we lead, we are being watched and evaluated. Through our words and actions, we reveal our character and our beliefs. We have a responsibility for those we are leading, both formally and informally, to be authentic in our leadership and to never abdicate our duty. We can endeavor to be firm, fair, flexible, and forgiving in our interactions and relationships as a leader, irrespective of whether it's in the workplace, in our church, or, most importantly, in our homes. The people we lead will fail and they will make mistakes, and as leaders we will need to hold them accountable while doing our best to follow these principles. When we ourselves fail or make mistakes, we should hold ourselves accountable but also apply those same principles to our own situation. Stand firm in your beliefs, be fair with your judgment, be flexible in your decisions, and be forgiving in your relationships.

CHAPTER 10

Next Man Up

Ask anyone who knows me, and they will verify that I am a huge sports fan. Therefore, a lot of what I relate to and enjoy revolves around sports and trying to stay in shape. If you follow any sport, especially collegiate or professional sports, you will often hear coaches, players, or commentators use the phrase "next man up". It is typically used when a starting player is injured and the second-string player in that position, or a bench player, is called to take their place. That mentality and culture is an integral part of high performing players and championship caliber teams.

It should be no different in our EMS organizations. We need highly motivated people who are willing and ready to step up when they see a job that needs to be done, a mission to be completed, or an opening vacated by someone who filled a vital role. We often use team concepts in our educational offerings, during our skills stations, and in our simulation training. In areas struck by or expecting disaster, or in need of specific response capabilities, we may send specialized strike teams to meet these needs or to augment local response. We even use a form of this team concept, albeit on a smaller scale, when it is only us and our partner on the ambulance. We must work together as a team to be successful and to provide the best care for our patients. Some of the organizations I have been part of have been great at the team approach, and others were deeply fragmented with no sense of purpose or goals. The fragmented groups often found themselves sitting on the sidelines waiting for someone else to step up.

For our organizations or teams to be successful, we must find ways to encourage the "next man up" mentality and we must model that in ourselves as leaders. Especially in EMS, there is no room for "spectators" who are going to sit idly by and wait for someone else to fill the gaps. The high performers in our organizations are those who will find work, even if it is something as simple as taking out the trash at the station, washing the dirty dishes that aren't even theirs, or spending extra time with the new EMT student helping them learn where all the equipment on the ambulance is located. They will speak up when they are closer to a call even though they may have run more calls than anyone else on shift that day. They are always on the lookout for ways to grow, advance, and serve.

The best way to encourage this type of mindset, and to grow it in your team, is to model it with your actions and behaviors. You must also acknowledge your team members' efforts when you see it in action. I would daresay that a great number of leaders were put in their role because they were great doers. I know that was the case for me. I have always been one of those who wanted to jump in with both feet in any situation. I wanted to be first during training scenarios in paramedic school, and at work I would be looking for the small, seemingly menial, jobs to do around the station. I have been known to trim the hedges, fix damaged walls, strip and wax the floors, and even make minor repairs to the ambulance. My bosses always knew they could call on me anytime to get things done. I tried to carry that forward and continue to model that mindset throughout my time as director. I have found that my willingness to do the small things has been contagious at times, and has helped foster growth in many of my team members.

"For it is better, if it is the will of God, to suffer for doing good than for doing evil" 1 Peter 3:17 NKJV

One of my best examples of the "next man up" mentality occurred in October of 2018. Weather reports were forecasting landfall of a major hurricane in Florida's panhandle. In anticipation of the potentially devastating effects of a Category 5 hurricane, Florida Emergency Management made an Emergency Management Assistance Compact (EMAC) request to Tennessee for ambulance strike teams. They asked for these teams to respond and stage near the expected impact, but in a safe location. This is a common occurrence when a major disaster is expected to overwhelm local capabilities.

At the time, I was the Ambulance Strike Team Coordinator for our region in Tennessee. Therefore, when the request was received by our state EMS office, they called me and the other regional strike team coordinators to see if we could pull our teams together for the response, with departure times scheduled in the next 24-48 hours. For those who are not familiar with an ambulance strike team, it is minimally made up of five ambulances, 10 EMS providers, and a team leader with a support vehicle.

As I communicated with our state EMS consultant, Steve Hamby, and our regional EMS agencies that participated in the strike team, we realized that, due to staffing issues in some agencies and ambulance shortages in others, we would only be able to put together a team of four ambulances and a team leader. One of the agencies had agreed to send the team leader and, to have at least four ambulances from our region, I agreed to fill one of the ambulance crew spots. I would partner with one of my other paramedics, Steve Helton, taking one of our Jefferson County EMS ambulances and letting the supervisor from the other agency be the team lead. The state consultant advised that another region had six services to volunteer ambulances, so they would attach their extra crew with our strike team. The next morning, we received our orders, loaded our gear and extra supplies on our ambulance, and we set out to rendezvous with the other teams from across Tennessee later that day.

In all there were three strike teams from Tennessee, geared up and ready to head straight toward an anticipated category 4 or 5 hurricane named Michael. We rallied with a total convoy of 15 ambulances, three team leader vehicles, two state EMS consultants, and a support vehicle with a mechanic. Our plan was to travel to Troy, Alabama, which was supposed to be northwest of the anticipated track of the eye of the storm. The state had arranged with a local fire department to feed us and give us a safe place to stay overnight so we would be within effective range to respond once the hurricane passed.

The entire trip I kept monitoring the storm and the weather forecast, and began to realize the storm was growing and moving a bit faster than expected. We had uneventful travel until about an hour outside Troy, when we began to hit heavy rain and 50 mile per hour wind gusts. This slowed us, but we finally arrived in Troy after dark. Coinciding with our arrival in Troy, Hurricane Michael was making landfall near Mexico Beach and Panama City, Florida. The fire department had a good hot meal ready, for which we were very thankful. While eating, we were notified the plans had changed and they would need us to continue travel toward the expected landfall. Our new anticipated route should bring us in on the west side of the storm as it passed and turned northeast. As with any best laid plans, the unpredictability of these deployments force change, so we would not be sleeping in Troy that night.

We all loaded back in our ambulances, took on fuel, and pressed forward toward Florida. We moved onward, headed for the currently unknown damage from Hurricane Michael as it was making its way across the panhandle and into Georgia. The closer we got to the Alabama and Florida border, the more wind damage we began to see. We began to encounter tree limbs and other debris in the roadway, so the whole convoy was on alert and there was constant communication from the point vehicle to the rest of the group.

Before entering Florida, we were informed by Mr. Hamby that our team had been requested to divert to a small hospital in Marianna, Florida that had received damage and needed evacuation. Apparently, we were the first out-of-state assets to arrive, and we were the closest to that facility. We eventually had to leave the luxury of the four-lane highway we had been travelling on and venture into the unknown darkness of a two-lane roadway in what seemed like the middle of nowhere. We had not even traveled a mile when we began to encounter multiple trees blocking our path. We passed them in the opposite lane or any place we had room to maneuver around, or we stopped and the lead team would cut and clear any trees that were impassable. We were now one huge traffic jam on a rural highway that had probably never seen a traffic jam throughout its existence. It was extremely stop-and-go in the black of night. Due to power outages, the only light source was our vehicle headlights and we were in a place where none of us knew exactly where we were.

While trudging along, we had been battling the downed trees for a couple of hours when the silence on the radio was broken by Mr. Hamby. He informed the entire convoy he had received a call from Florida's Emergency Operations Center, and they had an urgent request. There was a pregnant female in active labor at a very small hospital/clinic in Blountstown, Florida, about 50 miles south of our current location, and our team had the closest ambulances available. Mr. Hamby asked if any crew wanted to volunteer to leave the strike team, go it alone, and try to make it to the small hospital. There was a protracted pause on the radio. I knew we were one of the few crews that had a satellite phone and onboard internet, and I felt confident I could route us there if we could find a clear path. I looked at my partner and asked if he trusted me and felt comfortable with us trying to make it, and he said he was up for the challenge. None of the others were speaking up, so I radioed Mr. Hamby and said we would step up and try to make it to transfer this OB patient. Little did I know what I had volunteered us for.

My partner, paramedic Helton, maneuvered the ambulance out of the stack and finally got us turned around on the little highway so that we could journey on our own to our new destination. It was approaching midnight, but we forged ahead. We made it back to the four-lane so we could travel further south and then turn on a different two-lane highway to head east toward Blountstown. We immediately encountered the same situation the rest of our team had been working through earlier. Luckily, there was a forestry strike team in front of us clearing a path, and we thought we had hit the jackpot even though it would be slow. Little did we know they were clearing a path to their staging area for the night, which was only a few miles down the road. Once they reached their destination, they turned, and we knew we were in for a long 20 or so miles.

Steve needed a break from driving, so we swapped out and pushed forward into the darkness. It was an eerie feeling being in an unknown area with no contact with resources and navigating around downed tree after downed tree. By the grace of God, over the next couple of hours, we were able to navigate our way to the tiny hospital. I must say it was an adventure and the hospital we arrived at was not what I was expecting.

It was more of a clinic than anything. It was staffed by a few nurses, a nurse practitioner, and a respiratory therapist. They were managing two ER beds and about six in-patient beds which were all full. It was 4 am by the time we pulled into the ambulance loading area and made contact with the staff. They were excited to see us, as they did not know the EOC had found anyone to come help. They were even more surprised we were from Tennessee. We met with our patient and found she was in labor but was stable, and the delivery was not as imminent as we had been told when we were requested. We discussed with the patient and the staff the situation with the roads and the fact we had now been up for almost 24 hours. We thought it would be best to wait a couple of hours for daylight before we tried to make it the 60 or so miles to Tallahassee. We all agreed that was the safest option.

After I got enough satellite signal to contact Mr. Hamby, I informed him we had made it safely and what our plan was, Steve and I retired to the ambulance to try and get a couple of hours' rest. Steve took the cot and I took the bench seat. In case you ever wondered, it is not very comfortable trying to sleep in the back of an ambulance, especially when your partner snores. However, we were both exhausted, so we did eventually fall asleep.

Those couple of hours went by too fast and the sun came glaring through the back window of the ambulance, alerting us it was time to get moving with this expectant mother. We got her loaded and ready for transport and I agreed to do the driving on this part of the journey. We encountered many of the same obstacles of downed trees and powerlines during our attempt to get to Interstate 10, which we hoped would be our best route to Tallahassee. It was much easier and less nerve-racking, navigating the hazards in the daylight. The transport, while much longer than it normally would have taken, was uneventful. We arrived at Tallahassee safely and dropped of the expectant mother with the ER staff, with the baby still not delivered at that point. I feel compelled to add the staff at the trauma center in Tallahassee was handling this disaster with great composure and I could tell they were well prepared. They treated us exceptionally well, knowing we were far from home in a strange new place, and they made sure we knew where we could get some refreshments and rehydration. We cleaned up and waited to meet our team as they brought the evacuees from Marianna to Tallahassee.

In all, we spent 10 days in Florida. The first few days we spent our nights in a parking lot in Tallahassee. We would go out each day to help evacuate a nursing home or complete whatever assignment was needed. Eventually our three Tennessee teams were sent on different assignments, and our five ambulances and team leader from our specific Tennessee region were sent to backfill a 911 service on St. George Island. They had suffered heavy damage and flooding, and their small agency had been going non-stop for days and needed some rest. The fire department put us up in a couple of their stations and we covered any 911 calls for the next week or so. It was a long 10 days, but we met some awesome people and felt our whole strike team made a huge impact. We had all answered the call to leave our families and go straight into a disaster to serve others.

    Steve Helton and I stepped up when a need was identified, we led by example, and we chose to leave the security of being with the whole team to serve someone in in a precarious situation. We did not do it to prove anything or say that we were better than anyone else; is the choices we made reflect the character and personality that Helton and I have in common. We see something that needs to be done and we do it. That small act of selfless service laid the groundwork for the rest of the team to be confident and step up to act during that entire deployment. There was some great work done by all the team members and the team leaders. We made an impact on many people who were devastated by a major hurricane. So many people couldn't believe that a team of so many EMS providers would come all the way from Tennessee to help and they were exceedingly grateful.

    I have always been a "doer", never the one to stand back and watch others work. I have always tried to lead by example first and I try to instill that same mindset in those around me. Many leaders, no matter the organization, are promoted into their positions because they excel at completing tasks. The downside to that personality trait is that it can harm your growth and abilities as a leader. I have often done things myself that I should have given to someone I was leading so they had an opportunity to grow and learn. Not only does it deprive our team of opportunities, but it will also often pull us away and rob valuable time from the things we should be focusing on as a leader. I have, at times, been guilty of getting pulled into simple daily tasks when I had someone on my team capable and willing to do them. Nonetheless, I went ahead and did it myself, which eventually caused me to neglect a leadership responsibility only I could resolve.

I had to learn over time how to better delegate tasks to my staff, to give them the freedom and opportunity to step up and accomplish the goal. I needed to let them know I would not step in and take over their project, but I was there to mentor and support them if they needed it. That change in my doer mindset helped me to grow as a leader, made me a better mentor to my people, and helped the organization grow stronger. That did not mean I totally stopped being a doer. I still step up and fill gaps as I can to ease the load of my team. I want them to see they have my support; they are not on their own, and no job is too small for anyone. I have learned to temper and control it better, and I try to keep my leadership priorities in focus.

On any team we have members filling important roles and, as leaders, we have hopefully put the most skilled people in the roles where they can be most successful. At times the hardest part is managing that "bench player" or the second-string person. They may be young, or may have recently joined the team, and they don't have an official title other than EMT or paramedic. They need help to understand the organization and to begin to view themselves as the "next man up". At an early stage, we must start preparing them to fill someone's role as a preceptor, a field training officer, an instructor, a community outreach ambassador, or whatever appropriate position exists in your organization. If nothing else, they need help learning how to simply lead their fellow employees by example, and be genuine in their words and character while performing our selfless service.

Being willing to step up and answer the call is something we are used to in EMS. It is part of who we are as a profession, and it is the nature of our business. But, like any team, we can lose focus and become complacent or lazy. If this occurs, we will not be prepared to step up when our number is called and we are needed to fill a critical role or become a leader. We must be vigilant in our craft, and we must watch and train to fill the roles above us should an opening or gap arise. As Christians we are all called to step up and act according to His purpose, to be willing to meet the needs of the least of these in our world. It is our calling, our purpose, and our duty to step up and serve.

CHAPTER 11
Point Man and Rear Guard

"And the Angel of God, which went before the camp of Israel, removed and went behind them; and the pillar of the cloud went from before their face, and stood behind them." Exodus 14:19 NKJV

      I have had the distinct honor and privilege to serve as a tactical medic for our Sheriff's Department Special Operations Team (SORT) for many years and I can surely attest to the importance of teamwork in that high-risk environment. While each person on the team has specific specialties and assignments, we work hard to cross-train and to understand every person's role on the team. We do this to not only be able to function efficiently and safely, but to also maintain operational readiness and effectiveness should a team member be absent or go down during an operation. While every person on the team has an important role, there are two key positions on all our SORT operations when making entry into a high-risk situation: point man and rear guard. I want to use these as examples of roles we as leaders will need to assume at various times based on the situation.

Brad on SORT Training

The Point Man

The point man on the entry team is in arguably the most dangerous position on the team. They are at the front of the rest of the team, typically carrying a ballistic shield in addition to wearing their body armor and helmet. They are usually one of the more experienced operators and are the first line of protection and defense for the entire team. Their role is to continuously scan ahead, watching for and calling out potential dangers and threats. The point man must communicate with the entire team regarding what lies ahead and guide each of them when to move or hold their position. The effectiveness and safety of the team hinges on the point man's ability to safely navigate through hostile environments.

The point man must have exceptional skills of observation, situational awareness, physical endurance, and communication. He must avoid getting tunnel vision on a specific entry point or area and must be continuously scanning in front of the team. His movement and communication dictates where the rest of the team will move and, if he takes the wrong steps, it could lead to the failure of the entire mission and, possibly, injury or death.

It is a huge responsibility, and some teams often change point men during prolonged operations, or from one operation to the next, to avoid fatigue or burnout from the stress of that responsibility. The team leader is usually not the point man because his primary role is to oversee the entire team and make tactical decisions on the move. If he is on the shield, he risks becoming target-focused, which would distract him from his duty to direct his team and relay information to command. However, occasionally due to movement or rotation of the team, the team leader may end up as the point man at some time during the operation. He must be ready and willing to step into that role when necessary for the good of the team and the success of the mission, all while using sound judgment on when to move back in the stack into his traditional role.

    As an organizational leader, we have hopefully put talented and dedicated people in important roles to be the tip of the spear. If we have done our jobs as leaders, we have empowered them to do their jobs and make decisions as necessary. However, there will be times and situations that a leader will need to step up to be the point man for your people. You will need to lead from the front, protecting and guiding your team through crisis situations.

    During my career as a leader, there have been numerous crises during which I needed to lead from the front and be the point man. As an organization, JCEMS has sadly had several actively employed colleagues die due to medical conditions, and we have tragically endured one line of duty death. Out of respect for their families, their stories are not mine to tell. However, every one of those losses were unexpected and hit our organization hard. I knew that how I responded to those losses would set the tone for the entire team. I needed to lead from the front and let them know I was there for them. I needed to help us all navigate safely through these events by taking the lead, shielding them from any dangers, watching out for their well-being, and communicating with them the plan and safe route to the other side of the tragedy. It was a role I gladly accepted, but there were many times the shield was heavy and I grew weary myself. Thankfully my team was willing to follow me, trusted me to shield them, and was ready to support me when the shield became too weighty.

Being an executive leader does not require you to always be out in front as the title of "leader" would imply. As a matter of fact, it is not the most appropriate place for you to be all the time anyway. If you are always out in front, there will be times you are too close to the action. You will be so consumed by what you face that you will lose sight of the big picture and miss a problem that is further down range. We, as leaders, need to put our most capable people out front whenever we can so that we can distance ourselves from the point of attack. That way we can see the entire battlefield and push our team in the right direction for success.

The Rear Guard

It was 5 a.m. on a cool spring day when we gathered at the sheriff's office to be briefed on a warrant service we had been alerted to the night before. Our team assembled in the briefing room and checked our gear before the briefing started. I had only been on the team a short time, had recently completed my first SWAT school, and was eager to put my new knowledge into real-life action. As the team commander took a head count of team members there to respond, he began to delegate and assign tasks. A few of our team members had not completed all their training yet, so they were assigned to the perimeter. This is where I had spent most of my time on operations up to this point.

The team commander came to me and told me we were a man short and he needed me to be on the entry team today. He asked if I was ready, and I shook my head and said I would do whatever he needed. He said he would place me at the rear of the stack with my primary role as medic, as usual, but this time with the added role of rear guard on the entry team. We received our briefing on the warrant, the suspect, the structure we would be entering, and all the potential weapons and hazards that were known or suspected. We mounted up in our SWAT van and we were ready to roll before daylight.

It was about a 10-minute drive to the location and we double-checked our gear, and reaffirmed our roles and the assault plan, while riding toward the address. There is always a little extra adrenaline pumping through my veins the closer we get to the scene of any operation, but I was calm and ready. The driver yelled "30 seconds out" and the point man and team leader opened the back doors of the van to prepare for dismount.

We came to an abrupt stop and began to exit the van. I was naturally the last out due to my designated position on the entry team. We rallied behind the point man and moved in our stack toward the front door to knock and announce. As the point man's first foot hit the front porch, I heard the "BOOM" as the sound of the flash bang echoed off the house. If they did not know before, they knew now: we were here. As the rear guard, my weapon was trained on one of the windows that was behind our team's position in case someone tried anything foolish or made contact from that location. The point man banged on the door, and the team leader announced we were with the sheriff's department and we had a search warrant. There was no reply from inside. The team leader yelled "breacher up", and the breacher unloaded his fury on the door with a ram, causing it to come completely off the hinges. The team rapidly moved inside and I followed, making sure no threats emerged from behind us that would put me or my teammates at risk.

    As the team moved through the house, we began to encounter more individuals than we expected from the intel we had. That taxed our team capabilities and tied up most of the entry team securing those extra people. My role as rear guard was now to hold the hallway that led to the remaining bedroom and to protect my team from the unknown threat area until someone could free up to assist in clearing the remaining room. As fate would have it, while the team was securing the three suspects, our primary suspect suddenly emerged from the back bedroom. He was not happy we had rattled him out of bed and obliterated his front door.

    I immediately began giving him the verbal command to show his hands and get down on the floor. I guess he did not realize I was the medic since I was dressed like the rest of the team, and I had my rifle pointed straight at him. Maybe I did a good enough job of using my authoritative voice because he quickly complied. My team leader had heard me screaming at the male to show his hands and he quickly emerged from the bedroom to secure the suspect. After the male was cuffed and detained, the team cleared the remainder of the house and we rallied outside to hand over the apprehended individuals to the patrol officers and to quickly debrief.

We went over some areas we could improve but, overall, the commander was pleased with the way things went. More importantly, we had apprehended the suspect and no one got hurt. The team leader pulled me aside after the team debrief and told me he was glad I had performed as I did. He affirmed I had prevented the team from a potential failure by not getting sucked into the room with multiple suspects, and that I had held my position guarding their backs. He told me if I had not done my job, the suspect could have gotten behind the team and put them in harm's way. I think I earned a bit of respect from the team leader and the whole team that day, and was no longer viewed as "only as the medic". I was honored that the team knew I had their backs.

As a leader of an organization, we are only as good as the team we have around us. Any functional team must rely on trust, and that trust starts with the top leadership. Not only must we trust our employees to do their jobs, but our employees need to be able to trust us as leaders. They need to know we stand behind what we say, they need to see that our actions reflect our standards and principles, and, most importantly, they need to know we have their backs.

We can develop their trust that we will be their rear guard, watching for any hazards that may approach from behind. While we most commonly face things head-on, there are things we potentially miss along the way that can come up to bite us later. Maybe we notice one of our team members is growing too quickly, becoming overconfident and taking unnecessary risks. We can have their back by helping them recognize this boldness, and understand the risks they are taking and the potential consequences of their actions. We can have the back of the employee who has run a significantly traumatizing call by checking on them, sharing our own experiences, and providing counseling when necessary. We can stand behind our employees when they are falsely accused of some type of mistreatment or illegal action, we know they did not commit. We may recognize a team member is becoming withdrawn, is self-isolating, and their work performance is falling below par, and we can counsel them to help with whatever life event that is negatively affecting them. When we have empowered our frontline leaders to make decisions and direct the team, we stand behind their decisions. This is true even if there are mistakes, if their intent to accomplish the mission was pure, and then we offer guidance only when necessary. There are many ways we can watch our employees' backs and, when we do, we build a significant degree of trust.

    The Israelites marched through the wilderness with God as their guide, we must have God as our point man. We must allow Him to guide our steps and help us navigate our lives. We must also trust Him to shield our backs from attack, as He shielded the nation of Israel with a column of smoke as they fled the Egyptian army and prepared to cross the Red Sea. When we know and trust that God will protect us, we are not afraid to follow Him and face the storms of life because we know He will guide us and He has our back.

As an executive leader of an organization, we must not forget our primary role is to be looking ahead, to have vision for the direction our team needs to move, to watch for hazards down the road, to develop an overarching plan, and to only be the point man when necessary. Most often we are in the command post, at a distance where we can have a wide view of the entire picture so that we can coordinate our team's purpose and focus. We must also remain close enough to the day-to-day activities that we understand the frontline needs.

There will also be times when we must have our employees' backs, helping guard them from issues they have failed to recognize and that attempt to sneak in from behind. The difficulty is being aware enough to know which role to be in and when. The flexibility of leadership, and the balance it requires of us, is one of the most significant challenges we face. We must discern when to step into each of these roles, as well as know when to transition out of that role and hand it off to someone else. I can tell you from my own experiences that filling these roles of point man and rear guard, when necessary, will build a strong bond of trust with your team. They will be more willing to follow your lead, thus ensuring mission success.

CHAPTER 12

Dark Days and Defining Moments

"But if a man lives many years and rejoices in them all, yet let him remember the days of darkness, for they will be many...."   Ecclesiastes 11:8 NKJV

Mass casualty Bus Crash Jefferson County, 2013

October 2, 2013, was one of those days in EMS and leadership that thankfully don't come often and that definitely leave a lasting impression on your life. I remember that day very well: it was a warm and sunny fall day, and I was out behind our station 1 working on the emergency lights on my new county-issued Tahoe. The tones dropped for a wreck on Interstate 40 for a bus crash versus a tractor trailer. I could tell by the timbre of the dispatcher's voice it was something significant.

The EMS dispatcher that day was one of my former paramedics, who was filling in part-time, and I knew he was not easily excited. He was calm and handling the call as professionally as possible, but I knew him well enough to tell by his tone that this was bad. Add to that I could hear the 911 lines ringing off the hook in the background of the dispatch audio.

Our initial two ambulances went enroute, with fire and rescue also responding. My Deputy EMA director, Tim Wilder, and the EMS Supervisor that day, Rodney Satterfield, were at the station with me and they went enroute immediately. I was frantically trying to reassemble my emergency lights, and I left enroute to the call a few minutes after my colleagues. As I look back, this was a blessing in disguise as it allowed me to process some of the initial information and get resources rolling our way before I got to the scene.

"Dispatch, this is Medic 7. We need every available ambulance in the county and as many helicopters as you can send. I don't know how many patients we have…. we have people lying everywhere." These were the words of the senior paramedic who was on the first EMS unit that arrived on the scene. That first radio transmission told me it was the real deal, and it was going to be a call like we had never answered before. I immediately requested mutual aid from surrounding counties and, by the time I arrived at the scene of the crash, I knew we had at least seven ambulances from other agencies responding. We also had four helicopters on the way to supplement the four ambulances we already had on the scene. As I exited my vehicle, I was hit by the gravity of the scene and I quickly discovered the description from the first paramedic was accurate.

We had a passenger coach bus on its side in the opposing lanes of the interstate, a commercial tractor trailer fully engulfed in flames, an SUV that had been pulling a boat smashed against the guardrail, and a column of black smoke visible for miles. I could readily see that multiple victims had been ejected, and our paramedics were already working their way through initial triage. Tim was coordinating with incoming aeromedical for a landing zone (LZ) on the blocked lanes of interstate west of the accident, and Rodney was coordinating a casualty collection point (CCP) so that we could better sort and treat patients. I met with fire command briefly to let him know I was there and to ascertain what additional needs we had.

The difficulty for me was trying to resist my instincts as a paramedic to be hands-on and care for patients. I had to focus on my duties as the senior EMS command. I found myself mentally drifting during the initial minutes of being on the scene. I left the command area to try to help a couple of the injured who had been ejected from the bus as we waited for additional personnel to arrive, knowing that as a leader I was failing my command responsibilities since this made me hard to track down. I handed off my patients to ambulance personnel who had arrived and, as quickly as possible, I went back to the command post. I fought my instincts and began to realize I needed to try and stay in one defined location so I could be more effective.

Soon after, I received word that we had a total of eight fatalities confirmed on scene, four critical who would go by air, eight more victims tagged as immediate who would go to the trauma center by ground, and two walking wounded from a passenger vehicle who were refusing treatment. I knew we had enough resources now on site to handle the patients and I could see my team working flawlessly in the CCP, performing lifesaving interventions in the middle of the blocked interstate. Once the injured were cared for and on their way, the lengthy process of caring for the eight fatalities began.

Though it was the largest scene that I or any of my team had been on, they performed some amazing work that day. If you queried the additional agency personnel who responded from EMS, fire, law enforcement, and our 911 dispatch, most would tell you it went more smoothly and more efficiently than we would have thought. Everyone stepped up, found work, and made things happen.

Once the emergency phase of the scene was over, the long process of investigation and cleanup began. Throughout the incident, the news media had been arriving, both outside the operational area and flying overhead. I knew that information requests, and the responsibility to put out accurate information, would fall to me. I finally got a second to stop and check my phone, which had been blowing up in my pocket. I had numerous missed calls from other EMS directors offering help, news media wanting information, and a call from my wife. If I may stop and suggest one thing to anyone who may find themselves in a leadership role at a large-scale scene, it is this: find someone to stay at your side with a notepad and give them your phone to screen those calls while you manage the scene. People are going to want to help, and information is going to need to be shared, so some calls simply cannot go unanswered.

I handled a few of the most important calls I had missed and then I looked around at our responders. They were hurting, tired, and battling a huge flood of emotions. I wanted them to have time to de-stress, rehydrate, get cleaned up, and, if necessary, go home for the remainder of the shift. The next 36 hours would be long, tedious, and absolutely exhausting for me and all the responders from that scene. I checked in with my supervisory staff and we developed a plan for checking on everyone before I left to address the media, as it was important to get traffic re-routed and initial information to the general public.

While driving to the media briefing, I remember feeling so inadequate, as if I hadn't done enough. Once again, I think I was fighting that deeply ingrained paramedic mentality of wanting to be the one using my skills, my knowledge and my hands, to help people. This is something I often find in many aspects of my leadership role, and it has been hard for me to delegate at times, especially in my early years as a director.

In the days and weeks to follow, I certainly replayed the whole scene, and the whole response, in my head. I kept trying to identify the things I could have done better and perhaps find a few things I had done right. I have always been critical of myself and have always had high expectations. Couple that with an inner child who often has low self-esteem and it can get ugly in my head sometimes. This tragedy was beyond anyone's control. That's a concept I learned pretty quickly in EMS, and I knew we had done everything in our power for everyone involved. But still I battled my feelings of personal inadequacy.

Every responder on that scene performed beyond all expectations and they deserve all the credit for the lives saved that day. It was many weeks later, while engaged in some passing conversations, I began to realize that maybe I did contribute to the success of my team. I had some colleagues who were not on that scene but said they overheard the radio traffic. They said they could tell the tone of the voices on the radio seemed to change once I began to make requests for resources and then set things in motion for additional assets once I arrived on the scene. They said they could tell everyone seemed a little calmer once they heard my voice.

I naturally shrugged it off initially, but later I went back and listened to the tapes and found perhaps there was some truth to what they said. It was confirmed even further when some leaders from other agencies approached me at a conference where I was presenting. They told me how impressed they were with how composed I appeared as they watched me work on the scene and then handle the press briefings. Again, I wasn't so sure because, to be honest, the whole time I felt like my mind was going 1000 miles an hour.

I have often described my actions that day as a duck swimming upstream, appearing calm on the surface and kicking like heck underneath. That calmness seemed to transfer to our whole team on that scene; they each handled the tragedy with great compassion, professionalism, and efficiency. I was proud to see them work together flawlessly and without any competitive egos. This was no doubt a defining moment for all of us as individuals and as an agency. It showed us what we could do in the most stressful of situations and that our education, training, and practice did hold value and that it paid off in the end.

The true realization for myself and my team regarding the impact they made did not come until months later. The church in North Carolina that owned the bus, and where most of the victims were members, came back and provided dinner for all the responders at one of our local churches. Several of the survivors came, along with family members of some of the victims who died were there. They all took time to eat and fellowship with those who had taken care of them or their loved ones in their darkest hours. There were some touching stories, and it was enlightening and healing for my team to hear from the victims' perspectives about what they had experienced and seen. As you might expect, there were lots of hugs and several tears that day, but it brought some much-needed closure for everyone. It provided a clear picture to our responders regarding the impact they made that day, and in fact make every day, that we often take for granted.

Thankfully calls on this scale are few and far between in most careers. When they do come, I can guarantee they will be a defining moment. If you are prepared and practiced, you have a dedicated team around you, and you remain calm and focused, you will succeed and make a positive impact. If you have been complacent, and you or your agency are unprepared, it will bring those inadequacies to light. At worst it could cost lives, and additionally it might end your career. Regardless of the outcome, you never want the feelings of regret because you could have done more for those that you serve. If you stay in EMS, or in any leadership role, there will be dark days you will have to walk through, and they will be some of your most defining moments. While they may not be as dramatic as this incident, the dark days will come, and they will come in many different forms, but I can promise that God will be with you. It will be your faith, focus, preparation, and planning that will determine the final consequences and define your leadership.

CHAPTER 13

The Burdens We Bear

"Shepherd the flock of God that is among you, serving as overseers, not by compulsion but willingly, not for dishonest gain but eagerly;"

1 Peter 5:2 NKJV

When you are called by God to be a leader, or you are placed in a position of leadership, it is not a responsibility that should be taken lightly. As a matter of fact, you should prepare yourself for the anticipated weight of the position, as it can be quite heavy and oppressive at times. There are numerous responsibilities that leaders, much like shepherds, must carry and balance to ensure those they lead are heading in the right direction, stay together as a unit, have their needs met, and know that someone will help protect them from danger or attacks. Leading others requires broad vision, dedication, vigilance, and patience. Most leaders carry more than those they lead could ever realize unless they themselves have walked in a leader's shoes.

In a likely apocryphal story that was popularized as a moral parable by the Roman philosopher Cicero, we are introduced to the character Damocles. He was a courtier of Dionysius I, the ruler of Syracuse, in Sicily, during the classic

Greek era. Damocles was responsible for attending to the ruler and his household. The story tells us that one day Damocles was exclaiming to his king how fortunate the king was because he, as a man with great authority, was surrounded by so many comforts and servants. We read that Dionysius offered to switch places with his servant Damocles for one day so he could feel the benefits of being king firsthand. Of course, Damocles was all for it. Damocles took his place on the king's throne and began to enjoy the lavish surroundings and being served by beautiful attendants.

Damocles quickly realized that Dionysius had arranged for a sword to be hung right over the head of Damocles during a sumptuous banquet. The sword was held in place by a single strand of hair from a horse's tail. This was meant to evoke in Damocles a sense of what it was truly like to be king. Dionysius wanted Damocles to understand that, although as king he had much fortune and luxury, the king always had enemies and dangers to worry about. He wanted Damocles to feel the constant anxiety of leadership, worrying about hazards that could remove him from his throne, and the uneasiness of self-doubt when making royal decisions that affect the whole kingdom. With that constant fear and anxiety literally hanging over his head, Damocles eventually asked to be relieved of his throne, as he no longer wanted the "fortune" of leadership. He realized that having everything you wanted at your feet could not affect what was above his crown.

King Dionysius effectively exhibited to Damocles the constant pressure a person charged with leading others can be under. As we examine this story, we must also clarify that Dionysius rose to power by committing many cruelties. This added additional anxiety to his reign, as he was in constant fear of the enemies he had created along the way. He also carried the weight all leaders carry, knowing that his decisions impacted everyone under his rule, and they were dependent on him for their well-being.

If you are currently in an established leadership role, I am sure you are already intimately aware of the burdens of leadership. If you aspire to be a leader in any organization, you must prepare yourself now and be ready to accept the burdens you will have to carry. Seek out successful and experienced leaders who are willing to share their struggles and who will allow you to learn from their experiences. That is part of the reason I am sharing the lessons I have learned, so that others might be stronger and be better leaders than I have been.

Those who have not sat in those chairs can never truly know the full weight of the position. Much like Damocles, we often see only the benefits and comforts that, we assume, those we follow are the benefactors of. Unless our leaders share their struggles, worries, and challenges with us, we have no true way of knowing everything they face each day. While in theory it would be great if we could let the people we lead walk in our shoes for a day, or be in our position for a day, it is virtually impossible. They would never feel the full weight of the responsibility because they would know the position was temporary and the ultimate authority would still lie with us.

What we can do is take our future leaders and let them shadow us and see the decisions we make every day. We can explain to them the process we use to make those decisions. We can be more open with our employees regarding our own struggles, worries, and frustrations, which will give them a glimpse into our world. However, until you sit in a position of authority or leadership, you cannot fully understand the weight and the precariousness of that station.

Whether you are a leader in your church, a supervisor, a middle manager, an EMS director, or the CEO of a huge corporation, the one thing that will elevate you from average to great is your motives. I have touched on this in several chapters, but it permeates all parts of our lives and our positions as leaders. When we value those who depend on us, and we truly care about their well-being, our decisions will be made with our employees' best interests at heart. The thing we must be prepared for with this mindset is that it exponentially increases the weight of the burdens of leadership. If, knowing this fact, you are still willing to accept the challenge, then you have already set yourself up for success.

As I have stated previously, I am far from perfect as a person and as a leader, and I have made plenty of mistakes. I also realize that I am not the first leader to make mistakes, and I will not be the last. I have been willing to own my mistakes and learn from them, thereby first leading myself. That is one of the first burdens of leadership I had to learn to carry, the reality that I was not always going to be right or make the right call. I first entered my executive leadership position thinking I needed to be perfect and that my employees expected me to have all the right answers. The reality was that no one expected me to be perfect; they wanted me to be honest and do my best to make things better for everyone under my leadership. Like a shepherd, they simply wanted me to watch out for them and guide them on the safest path. I also had to realize that when I did not make the right call, I had to stand up and accept the responsibility and consequences of my mistakes. Demonstrating to your team how you deal with the burden of imperfection, and exhibiting a willingness to own your mistakes, will build a great deal of trust and they will be more willing to follow you.

    A second burden we bear as leaders is the everyday realization of how our employees' quality of life can be so easily impacted by our decisions. This is analogous to how children's lives can be altered and impacted by the decisions of their parents or guardians. An employee's family and home life can be enhanced or harmed by their employer's decisions. Leaders must understand they will have to routinely make decisions that can influence the employee's ability to provide and care for their families. If we make a bad budget decision and overextend the financial capabilities of the agency, our decision could cost jobs and damage families. If we are detached and too distant from the daily duties of our staff, we risk overlooking vital ways we could make their jobs more efficient and less stressful. That work stress is often carried home with them and impacts their relationships and overall happiness. If they are not happy at home, they will often not be very happy or productive at work, thus the vicious cycle grows.

If we fail to look ahead to see future employee needs, and actively plan and recruit, we risk being short-staffed. We must realize this will overload our current staff, increase their stress, decrease efficiency, and potentially lead to losing the staff we currently have. If we deeply care for our staff, this is a weight we always carry. Each of our decisions should always include an evaluation of both the immediate and the long-range effects on our employees, as a whole and as individuals. This is a part of leadership I have always accepted and carried willingly, knowing the full weight of that responsibility.

One example of trying to reduce stress and improve the quality of life for my employees happened amid the COVID-19 crisis. We were several months into what I like to refer to as the "COVID craziness". Don't get me wrong when I use the term "craziness"; I am not downplaying its seriousness or devaluing any of those who lost their lives. I am acknowledging it was a time in history like none I had experienced, and it brought with it issues in healthcare that I had never encountered before. The stress on our providers was immense and their daily response load increased. There was constant change in requirements and standards for personal protection, additional disinfection and cleaning procedures, and shortages of supplies.

I worked daily to share any new information I could with our staff. I explored every conventional and unconventional supply chain for personal protective equipment and disinfection necessities. I knew my staff was worried more than they ever had about carrying home something to their families, so we explored all the options to make them feel safer. We were already facing some staffing challenges, and so was almost every EMS agency around us locally and, indeed, across the nation. The added stress and fear caused us to lose a few more employees and, during all of that, there were a few necessary terminations.

With all the contributing factors, the tension and strain on my people was palpable. I knew I needed to do more than provide good solid information and ensure they had all the necessary equipment. I was not confident there were enough quality providers available that I could hire to fill all the openings and, even if there were, it would take some time to recruit them. I needed to do something that would make an immediate impact and show my staff they were not alone.

I decided to start filling some of the open shifts on the ambulance myself to help ease the burden of call volume by not being short a crew. I informed my leadership team of my plan to fill the voids where possible, and I let them know this would pull me away from the office some days. Nonetheless, I felt it was necessary, regardless of the potential negligible impact on call volume made by one more ambulance. Where I hoped it would make the most impact was on my staff. I hoped they would see I was willing to get in the trenches with them and help carry the load. I wanted them to know they were not alone in this battle and that together we would find our way to the other side.

I typically would pick up a 24-hour shift on the ambulance, which would give me more days to continue to fulfill my administrative obligations. There were many occasions I would work straight for 36 hours or more before going home. I was not the only one who stepped up and worked long hours. There were numerous members of my field staff and management team who took on extra shifts to get the job done. That's what makes the team of professionals I work with so incredible.

I don't share any of this to brag on myself, but I found it to be a relevant example to highlight my point. During this time, I had several of my staff tell me how much they appreciated me helping them. This meant a lot to me that they noticed what I was trying to do. I also would get comments from crews from other agencies when they saw me at one of the hospitals. They would tell me how surprised they were that the director of a service was willing to pick up shifts on the truck and answer calls. I will say that I figured out rather quickly that, at nearly 50 years of age at the time, I did not recover as fast after long shifts as I did in my 20s. However, I do feel like my willingness to lead by example made a huge impact on my staff and even helped me recruit a few new employees.

A third problem that can weigh us down as leaders is the fact that, no matter what decision you make, there will be haters. Despite my best efforts over the years to make the best decision for my people and my organization, I have always had people second guess my motives or accuse me of being selfish. I have always worked to be fair and to do the best I could for the most I could. As a leader you are never going to please everyone all the time.

As a matter of fact, as a leader, it is a dangerous trend to direct our focus solely on people pleasing. There will be times when tough decisions must be made for the common good, and that will make some unhappy. As a leader, this is where we must do a better job of allowing the people we lead to see our thought processes and endeavor to understand how a decision is best for everyone in the long run. If we can help them understand our intent and why we made the decision, it can help temper their dissatisfaction. This is a burden with which I have often struggled. I have a high desire to achieve and want to do the right thing for my team, and I hate to disappoint people who depend on me. This makes it easy for me to become self-loathing and withdrawn when I perceive people to disapprove of my decision-making when I knew my intentions were pure.

I often spend a great deal of time in my decision-making process, trying to run each possible scenario and considering how it will affect all involved. Because I know the investment I have made in coming to those decisions, I have a tendency to take it very personally when I make a bad decision or if one of my team feels I did not consider how it would impact them. In EMS, the job itself is stressful enough without the leadership making it even harder. It has often been said that the average employee shows up thinking only about themselves, while a true leader shows up thinking of everyone else. This is a burden that can easily take leaders to their breaking point if they deeply care for their people, but it is a burden worth carrying.

A true servant leader never accepts the role or does what they do to receive any recognition or praise. We often carry our burdens in silent service to those we lead. Great leaders routinely take all the criticism because, ultimately, any individual failure can be traced back to some failure in leadership. Great leaders also tend to deflect and redistribute praise or credit for success because they know that, without the people they lead, there would be no success.

These are some of the attributes of a great leader I have tried to model and follow. However, it is human nature to want to feel appreciated. Regardless, more often than not in leadership, you will feel underappreciated, and this too can become burdensome. If you are like me and battle self-doubt anyway, it is easy to keep picking up those rocks that sometimes get thrown at us and keep putting them in our backpack to carry with us on our journey. Only other leaders can fully appreciate this burden of feeling undervalued for what you do. Some will say that carrying those burdens is "why we make the big bucks". I would say it is blatantly obvious that is not why I became a leader, because the weight of the responsibility far outweighs my wallet or bank account.

During my time as a leader, I have often personally added weight to my load to be carried. I care about my people, and they are each doing their best to live their lives and care for their families. And like everyone else in this world, life happens. They have struggles with finances, relationships, serious health issues, and loss of loved ones. In EMS there will undoubtedly be physical injuries and, unfortunately, some psychological injuries. When I know a member of my team is hurting or struggling, I have compassion for them. I catch myself trying to pick up some of their burdens and try to help carry the weight, thus making my load heavier. I am thankful for those who have allowed me to serve them in their times of distress. When I am able to help someone through a difficult time, it helps reinforce my purpose as a leader. Unfortunately, I have not always been able to help everyone in every situation, especially those with struggles I had no idea they were dealing with until after it was over. I have seen marriages fall apart, people lose their homes, responders suffer a career-ending injury, struggle with addiction, and leave the profession due to undiagnosed or unresolved PTSD. My natural tendency to want to help people has made this weight crushing at times, but it's part of what I was called to do as a leader.

Even though I have been a leader of a successful EMS agency for many years, my experience pales in comparison to those at much larger EMS agencies or large corporations. The larger the organization, and the more people you lead, the heavier the burdens can be. I can't imagine what a pastor of a large congregation feels as he carries the burdens of leading and protecting his flock. Nor can I fully understand the pressure a corporate CEO feels as he considers the effects his decisions will have on the hundreds of employees under his charge. What I can tell you is that I have carried, and continue to carry, several burdens daily, and that no matter what size the organization, the weight of leadership can be heavy. Thankfully there is a source of never-failing strength, and that source is our almighty God.

It is expressed throughout the Bible, but I routinely reflect on one of my favorite verses, Isaiah 40:31 NKJV, "But those who wait on the Lord shall renew their strength; they shall mount up with wings like eagles; they shall run and not be weary; they shall walk and not faint." No aspiring leader can ever truly know the weight of the burdens of leadership, but we can watch, listen, and learn from those we follow until our appointed time to lead. Once in a leadership role, we should turn to God for our strength and understanding, and the load will be much lighter because He will help us carry it.

CHAPTER 14

The Seeds You Sow

"Do not be deceived, God is not mocked; for whatever a man sows, that he will also reap." Galatians 6:7 NKJV

We are all walking our path and, hopefully, we are following the path that God has laid out for us to fulfill His purpose. As we walk our path, each of us sow some type of seeds with everyone we meet. Everywhere we go, we can sow seeds of harmony or seeds of discord.

Growing up on the family farm, my childhood memories are full of times spent in the fields and in the garden planting and harvesting crops. When we planted crops, we always made sure to know what seeds we were sowing, and we hoped those seeds would yield a bountiful harvest. We would clear and prepare the ground, and cultivate and care for the young seedlings as they emerged and grew. If everything went as planned, we would get the opportunity to reap the harvest that started as tiny seeds.

As leaders, we are sowing seeds in people. We nurture and coach them, helping them to mature and hoping the fruits of our labor will yield skillful people who will strengthen and sustain our organization. In Matthew 13, we read the words of Jesus as He tells the parable of the Sower. As the Sower spread his seeds, some of them fell by the wayside and the birds carried them away. Some seeds fell on stony ground, without much rich soil, and they sprang up quickly but then withered in the sun. Yet other seeds fell among the thorns, and the thorns sprang up and choked out the good seeds. Other seeds fell on the fertile ground, and those are the seeds that thrived and yielded a bountiful crop.

Every organization is made up of diverse individuals, each with their own personalities, backgrounds, and beliefs. Each of our people is at a different point on a spectrum of experience, from novice to skilled expert. No matter what their circumstances, our people are our field in which to sow our seeds of compassion, respect, honesty, trust, teamwork, service to others, mentorship, forgiveness, and any other of the core values of our organization. As expressed in Jesus' parable of the Sower, the condition of the "ground" the seed falls on determines what fruit, if any, the "plant" will yield.

In Matthew 13:19, Jesus tells us the seeds that fall alongside the path are those who hear the message about God's kingdom but do not understand it. This makes it possible for the evil one to snatch away what was sown in their hearts. In our organizations, this will most often occur because of our own leadership failure. We can fail to make our message clear and concise so that every member of our team, at all levels, is capable of understanding and applying the message. If our communication is poor and not easily interpreted, confusion will reign, and the message will be lost or the goals not reached.

Verses 20 and 21 describe the stony ground as those who hear the Word and quickly receive it with joy but, because they have no roots, they last only a short time; when trouble or persecution comes, they fall away. Often in our organizations we have young or new people who join our team and come in with great enthusiasm. They are eager to learn and be a part of the team, and they quickly adopt the principles of the organization. If we fail to cultivate that enthusiasm and don't "remove the rocks", they will begin to stumble when they encounter adversity or trouble. If we do not mentor them properly, they will wilt and crumble under the everyday pressures of life and the stresses that come with any profession. We must properly prepare the ground, doing our best to remove the stones, so that these people have room to establish roots and grow, lest they wither away and yield no fruit.

In verse 22, Jesus describes the seeds that fall among the thorns as those who hear the Word, but the worries of life and the deceitfulness of wealth choke out the Word and make it unfruitful. There are many thorns that can take root in our gardens and the gardens of our people. These include weeds of complacency, arrogance, overconfidence, unfaithfulness, selfishness, and conceit. As an unattended garden will be overtaken by weeds, so too will unaddressed issues take over our people. If allowed to take root, these character flaws will begin to overwhelm even our best and most experienced team members. If this occurs, it renders our team members, and the mission and vision of the entire organization, ineffective.

"But the seeds falling on good soil," Jesus says in verse 23, refers to someone who hears the Word and understands it. This is the one who produces a crop, yielding many times over what was sown. We all wish our organizations were full of these "good soil" people, as it would make our jobs so much easier. These individuals understand our mission, vision, and goals. They take all the information, support, and cultivation we provide, and they use it to produce good fruit. They are high performers and are the ones who ultimately not only make our organizations successful, but they make us look good as leaders. As we allow them a supportive environment in which to grow, they will in time begin to create and sow their own seeds.

As previously mentioned, my family and I always tried to make sure we planted the right seeds to yield the crops we desired. In our organizations we must always be aware of the variety of seeds we are sowing. We sow seeds in our people through both our actions and our words. While we may strive to sow good seeds that yield high quality people, we can, at times, unintentionally sow seeds of doubt, distrust, jealousy, anger, or strife. As leaders, we must be self-aware regarding what we say and do, and what message we are sending to our team. Are we sowing good seeds or are we sowing weeds that will take over the field and lower the yield of the harvest?

I don't think any leader who desires the best for their team ever sows weeds intentionally, but it does inadvertently happen. I know I have unintentionally sown some weeds along the way down my path of leadership, and they are hard to get out of the garden once they take root. Thankfully, there have been more times when I sowed seeds that yielded a bountiful harvest and led to other seeds being sown.

We may never realize how many seeds were planted and we may not realize where they all landed. Hopefully, at some point in your journey, you will have the experience in which one of those people in whom you planted a seed will come back and express the impact you had on their journey. That is what makes it all worthwhile.

For me one such occasion came many years after a seed was sown, a seed I did not even realize I had sown. Rick Slaven, who was one of the paramedic students I had precepted way back when I was a young paramedic myself, came to me some 25 years later and expressed how much the time he spent with me had meant to him. Rick has far exceeded anything I have ever done professionally. Among his many talents, he is a Critical Care Paramedic, a Paramedic Instructor, and has culminated in his educational journey by achieving a Doctorate in Education.

I told Rick, first and foremost, his success is his own and that I would never attribute anything I had done to his accomplishments. However, I did value his appreciation of the time we spent together and it was humbling for me to know I had left a positive impression on him during that short time on the ambulance. I am not sure he realized it at the time, but he was one of the first paramedic students I precepted, and I was learning from him as much as he was from me on those clinical rotations. He was teaching me how to be a better preceptor and a better leader, which helped propel me down my own path to leadership. The relationship I have with Rick, as well as many other students and employees I've worked with in similar circumstances, are some of the ones I value most. They give me great joy and pride in knowing that, in some small way, I have made a positive impact on others and have been able to fulfill a part of God's purpose.

As Christians we are commissioned by God to spread the seeds of the gospel of Jesus Christ. In Matthew 28:19-20 NIV, Jesus commands his disciples, "Therefore go and make disciples of all nations, baptizing them in the name of the Father and of the Son and of the Holy Spirit, and teaching them to obey everything I have commanded you. And surely, I am with you always, to the end of the age." As He explains in the parable some seeds will grow and others will fail to bear fruit, we may witness to someone directly by telling them about the gospel or we may witness to them indirectly through our actions and deeds. We may not get the blessing of seeing a seed we planted grow and produce fruit, but we must be faithful to sow those seeds and let God reap the harvest.

As leaders we are responsible for cultivating a vision for our organization. We must delineate where to plant our garden, what we want to plant, and what fruit we want to harvest. It is our responsibility to ensure we have the right seeds to sow by being self-aware. We must also be accountable to God and to ourselves with strong beliefs and principles. Secondly, we must find the most fertile ground in which to sow these seeds, with people who are willing to learn and who support the mission and vision we have for the organization. Next, as we find those people who are willing to be nurtured and to grow, we must put in the work to encourage good habits. We must help weed out any bad behaviors, mentoring and supporting them until their roots are established and the healthy plant can yield its fruits.

    Any farmer who is worth his salt will tell you that, with a bit of hard work, you can take almost any type of ground and grow a crop. It is simply a matter of whether the yield is worth the effort. It's our job as leaders to do our best to select the right people, work hard to cultivate each of them, and be willing to, when necessary, remove any weeds that threaten to negatively affect the yield of our team. Leadership is a labor of love, but in time it can produce some of the best tasting fruit. I have been fortunate and blessed that many of the seeds I have sown have branched into their own fields and continue to multiply the harvest.

CHAPTER 15

Wielding Your Sword

"Hide me from the secret plots of the wicked, From the rebellion of the workers of iniquity, who sharpen their tongue like a sword, and bend their bows to shoot their arrows of bitter words,"

Psalms 64:2-3 NKJV

Throughout the bible the tongue is portrayed as a two-edged sword. Scripture after scripture gives us warnings of the traps and trouble that an uncontrolled tongue can drag us into. I think we all know that our words truly matter, and that they can be used for good or for evil. I can assure you I have not always chosen my words, or the way they were delivered, wisely.

If I asked each of you to raise your hand if you have ever been verbally attacked, talked down to, bullied on social media, or had lies about you spread behind your back, most everyone would raise their hand. Especially if you are in any type of leadership role, whether it be in your workplace, church, or community organization, I know you have. We all have had encounters with those who wield their swords like reckless barbarians, destroying everything in their path.

As a leader, I have had my share of encounters with those barbarians always looking for someone to blame or attack. They often lurk in the shadows of our organizations, going from person to person searching for an audience or co-conspirators to join them as they spew their dissatisfaction, rumors, and lies. We must realize these types are everywhere and, if you are having a modicum of success in any part of your life, you will likely come under attack.

First, we must remember we can't control what people say. Second, what people say about us should not define who we are. It is how we treat people, and how we respond to our attackers, that defines us. We can certainly stand up for ourselves in an appropriate way by addressing any lies or untruths, but we must guard against lowering ourself to their battlefield where they are probably much more experienced. We can't allow ourselves to get caught up in the rumor mill or a retaliatory attack on our detractor's character. We have to let our actions speak for us and know that the naysayers will soon be seen for who and what they are.

"Turning the other cheek" is not always easy, especially when the attacks are harsh and untrue. I have had many instances when I wanted to lash out in return. That's my default, to give in to aggressive tendencies I have, and I continue to battle those internally. On several occasions my responses have come out in a most unkind and non-Christian way. The times I have turned the other cheek and let my actions and character speak for me; the verbal barbarians were eventually seen as their true selves and were ultimately defeated.

It is not only about how we respond to the word's others say about us. It is also the words we speak, and the interactions we have, with the people we encounter each day that reveal who we are and what our motives are. As paramedics, we routinely walk into people's homes and interact with patients and their families. We are often carrying our own personal emotional baggage that affects our body language, our speech patterns, and our tone. How we are perceived, and how we choose our words, can change the total mood of a scene. These things impact how confident the patient is in these strangers who walked into their life in their time of need.

I have known and worked with several paramedics who were great at their craft of prehospital medicine. They knew every skill to perfection, could recite protocols and drug dosages all day long, but could piss off a priest by only saying hello. I also knew paramedics who were barely average in their clinical skills, but they practically babied all their patients with the little comforts and polite attitudes. They were the ones who never got complaints, always got praise from their patients, and were known in our community as great paramedics. The old saying about "you can catch more flies with honey" or, to some in EMS, "catch more flies with BS", does hold true. I know I speak a lot about the bad calls, as they stick with us a little more. But if I'm being realistic, handholding and doing the extra little things to make our patient feel cared for is really all it takes on the large majority of our calls. It is most often those "handholding" calls where we truly make the most impact.

When we discuss awareness about our words and interactions, it doesn't only concern our patients. Everywhere we go we communicate with people, whether they are our coworkers, our supervisors, nurses, doctors, family members, the lady at the drive-thru, or the attendant at the gas station. Each of us, throughout the course of our day and our multitude of interactions, make statements and have conversations we don't even remember. We say and do things that have an impact on those we encounter. That impact can be positive or negative, but all interactions, regardless of how insignificant they may seem, leave some type of impression.

For example, we might stay on our phone while the cashier is ringing us up at the convenience store, never say a word to her, and never think twice about it. What we fail to realize is that this very cashier had 10 other interactions that day similar to ours, and every time it left her feeling more and more invisible and unvalued as a person. I myself have been guilty of such interactions. One of the things I continually catch myself doing is rapidly going from one task to the next, always focused on the next meeting or deadline, wrapped up in the sheer business of trying to get things done. I walk out of my office and past my coworkers and employees and barely slow down to say "hi." I don't mean to make them feel unimportant. However, I know at times I have made people feel that way. I apologized when I realized it, but I also know there certainly have been times I didn't realize it and missed the opportunity.

I also know from experience that not only what we say, but how we say it, makes a huge difference. Take, for example, an incident many years ago. I had been a paramedic for about seven years, and I was working my usual 24-hour shift with one of our newer young EMTs. We were dispatched to a motor vehicle crash with entrapment at one of our major intersections on a busy two-lane highway. We arrived to find a teenage male driver entrapped in a compact car from a T-bone collision with direct impact in the driver's door.

My partner checked the driver of the other vehicle and, when the driver stated he was uninjured, she immediately let me know the other driver was okay. I could now concentrate my whole focus on the young driver who was entrapped. While the fire department was stabilizing the vehicle for extrication, I climbed in through the passenger window to begin my assessment and treatment. The young man was unconscious, but his respirations were adequate at the moment. To complicate the matter, he had blood pouring from his nose and mouth. I knew I would need to protect his airway but, due to the entrapment and the damage to the roof of the vehicle, I couldn't gain enough access to do much more than apply a c-collar, insert an oral airway, and apply high flow oxygen. I then began to work on getting an I.V. so I would be prepared to treat him further once extrication was complete.

The firemen worked as fast as they could to get the roof off, which gave me more room to maneuver and allowed them to see what they needed to do further. The entire time I was in the car treating the patient, my partner was handing what I needed through the window and going back to re-check the other driver to make sure he was still okay. Once the fire department got the roof off, I was able to shift to the back seat and better access my patient. Then the firemen and I did our best to see what parts of the car continued to entrap the young man, and they came up with a plan to get him fully cut free.

While they worked to remove the door and roll the dash and steering wheel, I began to assist my patient's ventilations with a bag-valve-mask device, as his respirations were becoming shallower. I knew I needed a more secure airway and I needed to act quickly if this teenager had any chance of survival. Even though things were moving rapidly, it seemed like it was taking too long.

I realized the firemen were encountering difficulties with freeing this kid's legs simply due to the severe damage this high-speed impact had caused. I was able to get one of the firemen to pull the release to lie the seat back so I could decide if I had a decent shot at intubating from the back seat of this car. I saw that I had a good position, and the bleeding from the patient's nose and mouth had mostly stopped by now, so my chances of getting this intubation on the first try were good. I looked up to ask my partner to get me the airway bag so I could get the endotracheal tube and laryngoscope I needed, but she had stepped back to allow the firemen better access.

I could see her about 10 feet away, so I yelled for her to bring the items I needed, doing my best to override the noise of the extrication equipment and crunching metal. She quickly brought me what I needed, the intubation went as planned, and eventually the patient was freed from his entanglements. We moved him to the awaiting helicopter for transport to the trauma center, cleaned up our mess, and went back in service. Later in the shift we sadly found out the young man had died after arriving at the trauma center.

I thought we had done everything we could considering the severity of it all, and I thought my partner had done an outstanding job. Regretfully, I did not tell her that at the time. Other than the tragedy of the whole call, I never really thought much more about that wreck, as I had run hundreds of traumatic calls by this time in my career and many of them had resulted in fatalities. Therefore, it didn't really wind up in my mind's "trauma box," or any of the other permanent memory "boxes" I had created. What would eventually cause me to file it away in one of those "boxes" came much later.

Now you must understand that I am getting older, and my years in this business have filled up several of my "boxes", so some things are harder to retrieve than others. That being said, I am not sure how long it was after that call before that young EMT told me something that brought back the memory vividly. I am not even sure how the subject came up, but that probably doesn't matter. What is important is that she proceeded to tell me, "I will never forget when you yelled at me on that wreck".

Not having filed it into one of my "boxes" yet, I understandably replied, "What wreck? I don't remember yelling at you." She proceeded to tell me the details of the wreck at that intersection where I intubated the teenager from the back seat. I said, "Oh, now I remember that call, but I don't remember yelling at you". She said, "I remember it very well, because you looked up at me and yelled at me right in front of everyone on the scene, 'bring me the airway bag'". She said even the firemen asked her when the call was finished what she had done to make me mad.

I was floored. I told her I didn't recall being angry with her, and certainly didn't think I was yelling at her. I thought I was simply trying to project my voice over all the noise. I told her I was sorry, that I didn't mean anything negative toward her, and that I wished she would have said something to me that day when we cleared from the wreck. That conversation put that entire call, and the subsequent conversation, in my box labeled "casualties ".

I'm glad she eventually had the courage to discuss this with me. I am also thankful she did not let that interaction with me drive her away from EMS or from our agency. She went on to become one of our best paramedics and do great things in our organization. I have often reflected on that conversation and that call. She helped teach me that my words matter and how I deliver them makes a difference.

How I "wield my sword" has consequences; it can cause harm and inflict pain, or it can provide protection and make people feel secure and seen. As in this case, I have not always used my tongue responsibly. There are times I have lost my temper and said things that can't easily be undone or taken back. There exist numerous interactions where I have not paid attention to my body language or my tone, nor have I seen how those things affected what I was saying and how my message was received. I have failed to engage people when they have simply been seeking my interaction and input.

As I have gotten older and more experienced, I think I have gotten better at mastering my "swordsmanship". After that interaction with the EMT, I began to pay more attention to how I use my sword. I am more cognizant of who I use it on, how hard I swing it, and, most importantly, when to leave it in its scabbard. The tongue is a tricky tool and hard for us all to control at times. For those who don't learn to harness how they use it, it becomes a massive stumbling block and inhibits them from their potential and purpose. It causes them problems in their personal life, damaging relationships and marriages. In their careers, it holds them back and often costs them opportunities or even their jobs.

If you have worked in EMS or public safety for any amount of time, you have probably met at least one or two of these people along the way. We all know the coworker who is always grumbling, always annoyed with the world, and doesn't care what they say or to whom they say it. We all know that person who everyone says can't get out of their own way, and it's probably because they keep tripping over their own tongue. I reiterate that I am not an expert "swordsman"; I have tripped over my own tongue and hurt others more times than I care to admit. What I am saying is I am more aware of the impact my words, or oftentimes my lack of words, have on those around me.

We all can be more aware of what we say, who we say it to, when we say it, and how we say it. Colossians 4:6 reads, "Let your speech be always with grace, seasoned with salt, that ye may know how ye ought to answer every man." Our words matter, our people matter, and the impact we have on each other matters. So, I urge you to wield your sword responsibly!

CHAPTER 16

No Investment, No Return

"In a multitude of people is a king's honor, but the lack of people is the downfall of a prince." Proverbs 14:28 NKJV

Noted author and leadership expert John C. Maxwell has many books that share lessons on leadership and, over the years, I have gained considerable self-growth from his teachings. I regret I did not encounter and adopt some of his leadership principles earlier in my career, as I would probably not have made as many errors along the way. One of his quotes I feel is extremely insightful is, "He who thinks he leads, but has no followers, is only taking a walk." This gives us insight into the real purpose of leadership.

It is not about a title or a position in an organization or company. It is not about self-glorification or drawing attention to yourself and the authority you have. It is not about a leader's ability to tell others what to do. It is about the relationships we build, the influence we have, and the ability to empower others without us micromanaging them. If you want to have an exponential impact on your organization, and indeed the world, it will be accomplished through the influence you have. It will be achieved by you identifying high performing and reliable people and then developing them into leaders themselves. There is a maxim that states that the sign of a good leader is not how many followers you have, but how many leaders you create.

I have often heard the phrase used by leaders that "it's lonely at the top", but I want to emphasize it does not have to be that way. Even when we reach the top of an organization, our work is not done. In fact, it's only begun. Once we step onto the metaphorical platform at the top of our organization, great leaders begin to build onto that platform to make room for others to join them at the top. Those of us in leadership positions who continue to grow and advance ourselves must understand that, by developing others, we can multiply our investment, influence, and impact. If we are humble, focused, and work diligently, we can cultivate and nurture other leaders. The more leaders we develop in our circle of influence, the higher the performance of the organization will be. This also makes the burdens of leadership lighter for everyone because all the leaders share the load together.

When we invest our time, energy, knowledge, and love in our people, this is how we get a return on that investment. Growing other leaders is how all successful top-level leaders build their legacy. When a top-level leader eventually moves on to another stage in their life, their legacy will be defined by how they have influenced and developed those who succeed them. They develop people who can take their place, and not only continue the mission but surpass what has already been accomplished. In turn, these individuals will eventually grow new leaders themselves.

We can see key references throughout secular history and the Bible that support this concept. There are numerous examples of leaders growing other leaders and how it has an exponential impact. Look at the example of the Apostle Paul. God used him in the development of the early church and the spread of Christianity by mentoring and growing many leaders. One of the most notable leaders Paul influenced was Timothy. We read in both 1st and 2nd Timothy the letters Paul wrote to Timothy, giving him encouragement, instruction, and guidance on how to be a faithful leader. We observe his investment in leadership in each of Paul's letters to the different churches in Rome, Corinth, Galatia, Ephesus, Philippi, Colosse, and Thessalonica. Paul influenced and instructed numerous leaders who oversaw and led each of the early churches throughout these ancient cities.

Through Paul's example, we have a successful guide to cultivating other leaders. Paul first identified the people with the right character and gifts to lead and then he developed a relationship with them. Paul humbly led by example, showing strength and unwavering faith by sharing his failures and weaknesses. He then began to share his knowledge and empowered them by teaching them to intensify and use their God-given gifts. Then, as Paul grew these leaders, his investment was multiplied, as those church leaders began to grow their own leaders, thus creating a ripple effect.

In my own career, I have had many opportunities to work with, influence, and develop other leaders. When I first became Director of Jefferson County EMA and EMS, my management staff consisted of two deputy directors, one in Emergency Management and the other in the EMS division. Our EMS responsibilities were growing, and it became clear we needed further assistance to better manage operations and ease the load of my deputy directors. I requested additional funding and expanded our management team. I sought out experienced individuals with specific skills that compensated for some of my weaknesses. By doing so, I sought to strengthen the organization and make us more successful.

During the process of looking for the right people, I began to understand the importance of identifying others who desired to be future leaders. I knew we would have future needs, and I had identified a gap in that area. I began to develop a rapport with several employees who displayed leadership qualities, and I began to share ideas and thought processes with them. I encouraged them and gave them opportunities to grow by taking on projects that would teach them to lead. I have tried to mentor many employees over the years, and hopefully I have been a positive influence on their careers. Over time, we have fortuitously had additional opportunities to develop different leadership positions within our organization, which has helped us grow even more new leaders.

I recall one particular paramedic I began to mentor a few years after I became the director at JCEMS. He was young and very enthusiastic, always asking questions and eager to learn. I saw a great deal of integrity in him and that is something that has always drawn me to people. I witnessed his passion for the work we do and his genuine compassion for his patients. I related to him so well because I saw a lot of similarities to myself when I was a young paramedic. I don't know if he realized it at the time but, whenever I had the opportunity to stop and talk with him, I made a conscious effort to positively influence him. I sought to develop a relationship of trust and, hopefully, help him grow within our organization.

He was always asking me questions about decision making or trying to understand various thought processes. He sought to understand why things were the way they were and if there was a way to improve. I saw a great deal of potential in this young man, and I had high hopes for the impact he could have on our team. Unfortunately, at the time there were not as many opportunities for promotion in our organization. Despite my best efforts to provide this young paramedic untitled leadership opportunities, he eventually left for an organization that was much larger and had numerous advancement pathways.

When he told me he was leaving and told me about the opportunities he would have at the other organization, I totally understood and supported his decision. I was still disappointed, not in the young medic, but in myself for not finding enough openings to help me hold onto him. Ultimately, I knew this was what was best for this young man, and I knew he would be very successful. Many years later my confidence in him has proven to be accurate, as he has been very successful in the organization he moved to and has been promoted several times. He is a leader and mentor to other young providers in that organization and I hope they realize what they have.

Over time he has often come to me to ask for advice or insight into how I make decisions and how I lead others. He has also expressed to myself and others some of the things he has seen in my leadership he has learned from, decisions that I did not even realize anyone noticed. His compliments and respect have always been a source of encouragement for me, as I often only see my failures and not my influence. I want to emphasize that this young paramedic, and the many others I have tried to mentor who have gone on to be successful, have done so by their own talents and abilities. Their accomplishments are their own and I am not attempting to take any credit for their success. My only hope is that, in some way, I gave them support and the push they needed to slingshot them forward into an opportunity to succeed.

The first hurdle we must jump as a leader, when we want to build and influence other leaders, is our own ego and insecurities. This is especially hard for new leaders who have little experience in their role. It is hard to coach others when you are still trying to learn your position yourself. I struggled with this same problem when I was given my first titled leadership role.

It is common for new leaders to fall into one of two prominent traps. Some will be extremely overconfident, arrogant, and controlling. They must have their hands on every detail and they never allow anyone else to have the opportunity to learn or make decisions. Others will be so insecure about their own abilities they will never allow anyone a glimpse into their decision making. They keep everyone at arm's length and will not make any effort to encourage others to join their leadership platform for fear of exposing their own shortcomings.

There have been times along my journey when I slipped into both categories but, thankfully, found my way out of those snares. There are plenty of current leaders who fit both these categories and some of them are successful at running businesses and organizations. However, they never really advance into true leadership. They never invest in their people because they exaggerate their capabilities and expertise and think they do not need anyone else. Others tend to focus on hiding their insecurities and weaknesses. They are afraid someone may be smarter and more talented, or that their weaknesses and inadequacies might be exposed. To be a true leader, we must invest in our people. We must first be humble enough to share our knowledge, and thereby expose our weaknesses, with others so they can learn. We must be unselfish enough to show them we care about them as individuals and we want to help them maximize their potential. We must sweep our ego aside so we can make room on our leadership platform for others to join us and, perhaps, even surpass us.

The next thing leaders must do to develop other leaders and build their legacy is to identify and focus on the right people for the right role. Each of us is individually gifted with certain talents and traits. That is what makes our world, and our organizations, so diverse and interesting. As leaders we must be able to identify the special gifts of our team, which will enable us to place them in the best possible position to succeed.

The first step in that process is to develop relationships with the people we lead so we can begin to learn their strengths and weaknesses. We need to be able to observe them in various situations and assess how they perform. We cannot do that if we never give them opportunities to succeed or fail. All people have value because they are God's creation. Therefore, we must work with all our team to help them use their God-given talents to be successful. While we certainly want to develop leaders, not everyone is intended to be an executive leader. Some may only be meant to be leaders of themselves, quietly using their talents as an individual and serving others in their special way. Others may be gifted to be supervisors or managers of a smaller group. Some team members may be great communicators and their talents might lead them to be facilitators or educators in their organization.

We should direct our focus on each team member's specific gifts. We should invest in growing those gifts while mitigating any weaknesses that exist. In doing this, we give them an opportunity to succeed in fulfilling the purpose for which they were designed. Comparable to the stock market, we would not place our monetary investment in a low-performing company that is less likely to yield a positive return. We need to ensure we are putting people in the right positions and training them for growth into future positions they have the potential to fill. We certainly would not put a person in charge of an IT department who can barely open their own email. However, if that person is gifted in mechanical repairs, they may have the capacity to lead a maintenance department. As an executive leader who is trying to develop other leaders, you will have to focus your efforts in the right direction with the right people. Growing leaders is not easy and it requires time, valuable time that cannot be squandered. As an executive leader, you still have administrative obligations and duties you cannot neglect so, to grow your people, you will have to make sure you focus on the appropriate people and guide them to success. When our people succeed, our whole organization succeeds and will thrive long after we are gone.

Once you have humbled yourself and directed your focus to identify the right people for the right position, the real work begins. This is the investment you make as a leader and where you will receive the returns on that investment. As I have already said, it starts by learning and knowing your people and developing a relationship with them. Without a relationship there is little-to-no trust and, if you don't have trust, you don't have much at all. Without trust, you are not likely to invest, nor are they likely to be receptive to your coaching. I know in my own life the people I am most likely to listen to and take coaching or constructive criticism from are those with whom I have a close relationship. I am receptive because I know they care about what is best for me as a person.

Before we begin to develop other leaders, we must build a bond of trust with them so they will be amenable to our guidance and input. They must know that our investment in them is not for selfish purposes or to build our own ego, but that we truly care about them and their ability to maximize their potential. Most of us love to have people tell us the good qualities they see in us and the talents we possess, which is the positive side of mentoring. However, I do not know many people who love having their flaws and weaknesses pointed out to them, especially if we do not have a solid relationship with that person. This is the area in which we need to invest the most time to develop and mentor other leaders: relationship building. Getting to know who they truly are, their background, their passions, their fears, their gifts, and their weaknesses. We must also be vulnerable enough ourselves to allow them to see who we truly are, and where we shine and where we struggle. By sharing with each other, and being vulnerable with each other, we begin to build the foundation of trust upon which we can continue to build.

Once we have built a bond of trust and our relationship begins to grow, we can start to invest even more into mentoring the individual. First, we must let them know we see potential in them and express our willingness to mentor and coach them. Certainly, they can choose to participate and receive our offer of guidance, or they can reject it. Very rarely have I offered to mentor someone and have them refuse if I have put in the work to develop a relationship first. If they agree to being mentored, then we can begin to share insights into the areas of their personality that give them the ability to be a successful leader. We can also begin to identify their weaknesses, biases, and blind spots that could potentially trip them up or hold them back. We can begin to allow them to shadow us and participate in our decision-making processes so they can see firsthand what has traditionally worked.

We can begin to give them tasks and opportunities that push them out of their comfort zone while ensuring that, even if they make a mistake, we will support them if their intent is pure. They need to know that if they stumble and fail, we are there to help pick them up and guide them back on the right path. We must do everything we can to set them up for success, but give them enough room to make a misstep without falling to their professional death. We must also share with them not only our successes but allow them to see our failures. As I have discussed prior, none of us are perfect and the future leaders we mentor need to know that no one expects them to be perfect either. When we, as experienced leaders, allow our future leaders to see the good, the bad, and the ugly we have endured, they grow confident that they can be leaders too. I promise you if God can use this farm kid from East Tennessee to lead others, He can use anyone who is willing to follow Him.

One of my favorite quotes is from Robert F. Kennedy, "Each time a man stands up for an ideal, or acts to improve the lot of others, or strikes out against injustice, he sends forth a tiny ripple of hope, and crossing each other from a million different centers of energy and daring those ripples build a current which can sweep down the mightiest walls of oppression and resistance." We can begin to imagine how, as leaders ourselves, we can make ripples in the sea of life as we invest in developing other leaders. Our impact starts with a ripple that builds momentum in others and, as they begin to lead and invest in others themselves, those ripples multiply. This builds a wave that has an impact far greater than any one single accomplishment could. That is where we receive the return on our investments, not for our selfish benefit, but for the benefit of those we serve.

CHAPTER 17

Ask, Seek, Knock

"Ask and it will be given to you; seek and you will find; knock and the door will be opened to you. For everyone who asks receives; he who seeks finds; and to him who knocks, the door will be opened." Matthew 7:7-8 NIV

These verses are part of Jesus' teachings to his followers during the "Sermon on the Mount". In these verses he is describing how we should approach God and communicate our needs. Some might question why we need to go to God with our needs if He is omniscient and He therefore already knows what we need. However, He has ordained that we come to Him in prayer as His desired form of communication. Communication is part of how you build any relationship, and our relationship with God is no different. I am sure we all have been guilty at times of only going to God when we have a need and, when we do, we are the ones doing all the talking. We must not forget that proper communication requires listening also, and we need to be still and quiet and listen to His voice as it speaks to us.

Let me clarify my belief that when Jesus says, "ask and it will be given", this does not mean you will always get anything you ask for. If we approach God with selfish motives or a desire that goes against God's will for our life, He will not fulfill our request. We cannot use God as if He is a genie in a bottle, there to grant whatever wish we have. However, if we are in close communication with God daily, our desires will begin to align with His will and, thus, our prayers will be answered. When we seek God with our whole heart, setting aside our own wants and desires, we will find His purpose for our life.

This process of seeking is our way, as believers, to demonstrate acute awareness of God and His active guidance in our lives. Before all the technology we have today, if we needed something from our friend, neighbor, or even our boss, we would have to go to their home or office and knock on the door to make our request. This, I might add, is a lost art and a sign of respect missing in today's world. There are still some instances when we need to go in person to make a request. Out of reverence to, and respect for, God, we should approach Him in prayer and knock on His door. If we do so, He will open it.

You will notice these verses require action on our part. "Ask", "seek", and "knock" require us to go to God with our requests for our needs and His guidance. We cannot gain anything by sitting back and waiting for it to come to us. If you want to find your God-given purpose, you must seek God's direction. If you are facing difficulty and struggles in your life, you must humbly look to God for strength and comfort. If you desire to use your God-given gifts to change the world, you must knock on God's door and enter His presence so that you can intimately know Him and align yourself with His plan. As with all things, our personal and professional relationships should model the Biblical example of how we should interact with God. If we have a need or desire, it will require action on our part, but we must first establish a relationship of respect and trust before we make that request.

    It was another typical East Tennessee summer morning and the humidity was already on the rise. My partner and I made it our priority to wash the ambulance in an effort to avoid having to battle the heat and humidity later. Afterward we would typically try to make some breakfast at the station, and, on this particular day, I cooked some pancakes. We had finished preparing our plates and sat down to eat when the phone rang. Dispatch informed us we had a possible shooting victim. We left our plates and hurried out the door to respond to the scene several miles away. We traveled around the winding backroads as our siren broke the quiet calmness of the rural farmland that makes Jefferson County so beautiful. Typically, EMS stages in a safe location a short distance from the scene on a shooting call until it is deemed safe to enter. However, this time, prior to us getting to the area, the dispatcher advised that law enforcement was on scene and it was clear for us to go in.

    As we arrived, I climbed out of the passenger seat and grabbed the airway bag. An officer was standing in the doorway of the residence yelling at me to hurry. I was moving quickly, but we were taught to never run into a scene because that is when you will surely miss something that could get you hurt or killed. I made my way past the officer who was guarding the door, and he directed me toward the back bedroom where another officer was with the patient. As I walked in, I found a teenage boy lying on the floor with a single gunshot wound to the head. He had surprisingly little noticeable damage or external bleeding. The patient was still breathing and had a strong pulse but was unable to maintain his airway.

I began assisting with ventilations while my partner grabbed the endotracheal tube and laryngoscope that I would need to intubate the patient and secure his airway. As I looked into this kids' upper airway to find my landmarks, I noticed moderate bleeding draining into his oral cavity and down his throat, a finding which would definitely complicate the procedure. To add to this difficulty, this patient was still breathing some on his own and was involuntarily clamping down his vocal cords and clenching his jaw. Unfortunately, this was before we, as EMS field providers, had the ability to administer paralytics in what we refer to as rapid sequence intubation (RSI).

RSI was a protocol that aeromedical services in Tennessee had recently begun to use. Ground units in other states were also beginning to utilize the technique to aid in these situations. I had my partner request a helicopter, as this patient needed rapid transport to the trauma center. I attempted the intubation a couple of times in the house, but I continued to encounter difficulty overcoming the patient's involuntary responses. With each failed attempt, I would resume the assisted ventilations with a bag-valve-mask to reoxygenate my patient. Nasal intubation was not an option given the unknown internal head trauma, so I made the decision to move the patient to the ambulance. There we had a better space to work, and I at least had some diazepam (Valium) I could try to override the involuntary reflexes and aid in the intubation.

  Once we loaded the patient in the ambulance, I called the local ER on the radio to see if I could get orders to give this patient some high dose diazepam. We typically did not need orders for diazepam in seizure patients, but this was way outside any protocol we currently had. Luckily, when the nurse answered the radio, the ER physician was close by. Even more advantageous was the fact the physician was our EMS medical director. I told Doc who I was, and I quickly relayed what we had and that I needed to give this kid some high dose diazepam. He asked a few clarifying questions and told me to go ahead with the medication. It was the only option we had at this point since we were too far away from the ER, and the helicopter we had requested was still 15 minutes out.

  I administered the diazepam and, within a minute or so of bag-valve-mask ventilations, I was able to successfully intubate the patient. We proceeded to the landing zone and loaded the young man on the helicopter for transport to the trauma center. Once there, the trauma team determined that the brain damage from the bullet was too severe for survival. Thankfully the parents agreed to donate his organs; their loss possibly saved other lives and there would be something positive that came out of this tragedy.

This call, along with several other similar calls my colleagues and I encountered, revealed the need for a better protocol. While the high dose diazepam worked at times, it had significant potential complications. With the help of a couple of other paramedics, we began to research rapid sequence intubation and the use of paralytics in the field of EMS. I had discussions with my friends who worked at one of our local aeromedical services, seeking their input and opinion on the protocol. Once we had the information, we knew this would be the best option for our patients if we could get our EMS director and our medical director to agree. We knew it would be an uphill climb, but we were willing to put in the work. Some were reluctant at first, but we knew we had no chance if we did not ask.

I had developed a solid relationship with our EMS director, and our medical director had shown a great deal of confidence in me several times. Because of this relationship, I began to talk with them about the young man with the GSW I had treated some time earlier. Others in our agency were also working to share their experiences and advocate for change. Each of us was attempting to lay the groundwork for our request. As I told the story, I also shared my feelings that we needed a better way. I shared a couple of peer-reviewed articles with them to get them thinking more about the option. We knew we had to approach them with respect and allow them time to adjust to the thought of us being trailblazers in our geographic area. We would be one of the first in our region to see if this new protocol could be successful and better serve our patients.

My fellow paramedics and I continued to seek out supporting documentation, sample protocols, and success stories to present on behalf of adopting this new protocol. Eventually we had the opportunity to have a face-to-face meeting with our EMS director and our medical director to discuss a draft protocol and make a formal request. The EMS director was all for us being the first to implement this in our area. The medical director agreed this could definitely save some lives, but he had some concerns about training and skill competencies that we would need to address. Once we presented a comprehensive training plan, they both agreed to adopt the RSI protocol. I can gladly say that, over all these years since adopting this interventional protocol, multiple lives have been saved by our paramedics.

My colleagues and I had identified a need, and we knew exactly who we needed to approach to express that need. We had built a relationship of trust with the people who could fill that need, and we sought out their input and approval. We had trust that, when we approached them with our request, they would listen and would respond with the decision they thought was best for everyone involved. We had chosen to ask, seek, and knock with our leadership. We had made our needs known without selfish egos, but with a humble desire to better serve our patients.

In all things we should humble ourselves and seek God's face for His guidance and direction. He requires action on our part to come to him and acknowledge He is the Lord of all, and that He is our provider and refuge. Once we take action to ask, seek, and knock, we must be patient and wait on God's timing to fulfill our requests as He sees fit. However, we cannot sit back and expect Him to grant our every wish.

The same can be true in our professional lives. No matter what level we rise to in any organization, we will always have someone we answer to. We often must report to frontline supervisors, managers, bosses, investors, boards, or even politicians. It is imperative we build a relationship with those we answer to and rely on so that when we have a need or concern, we can go to them in good faith and make our request known. We need to ask, seek, knock.

If there is a critical piece of equipment or new process to make our job easier and more efficient, we need to act and **ASK**. If we want to bring about positive changes that will make our organization more successful, we need to **SEEK** the opportunity to engage our superiors to hear our ideas and guide us on the right path. If we desire to increase our responsibilities and advance our career, we need to **KNOCK** and see what doors of opportunity open for us. There is not much of value that comes in life without action on our part.

As leaders we have the responsibility to make sure we nurture those relationships down the chain of command, ensuring those who report to us feel comfortable coming to us with questions, concerns, or needs. We serve a benevolent and awesome God who desires the best for us. He can certainly provide for us without us asking if he chooses to do so, and He is always working for our benefit. Regardless, He desires a personal relationship with us. He longs for us to acknowledge His power and authority, turn to

Him in our times of need, and praise Him for the blessings we receive. It is imperative that we go to Him, not only in our times of desperation, but also in our times of blessings. We must act and we must ask, seek, and knock if we want our requests to be heard and fulfilled.

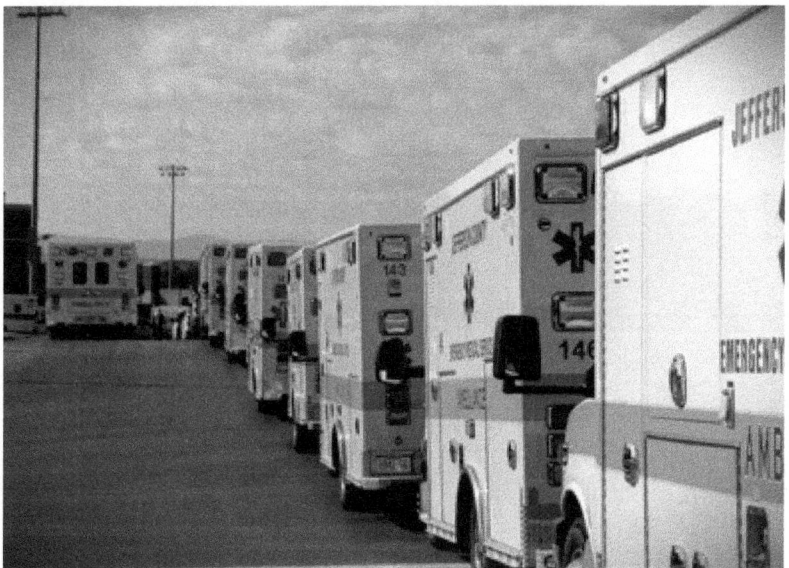

JCEMS fleet 2024

CHAPTER 18
Where Callings Intersect

In the book of John 15:16 NKJV, Jesus is speaking to his disciples when he tells them, "You did not choose me, but I chose you and appointed you that you should go and bear fruit and that your fruit should abide, so that whatever you ask the Father in my name, He may give it to you." This message still applies to us all today.

When I speak of answering the call of God, it is in reference to the process of identifying and responding to God's will for our lives. The primary call of God for each of us is to have a personal and intimate relationship with Him. We are expected to honor, worship, and follow Him by spending time in prayer and in study of His Word so we may be a light in a dark world.

We also have a secondary call to be disciples of Christ, going forth to teach all nations of His love and sacrifice for all who will receive Him. He endows each of us with specific talents and gifts that are designed to fulfill His purpose and that can be used in the service of others on His behalf. For many of us, that secondary call aligns with our given profession or vocation. Some have one singular purpose that God has given them the ability to meet. For others, He may provide multiple callings or opportunities, and those callings can even change with time or as a specific disparity or objective is revealed. Answering God's call can be a never-ending journey of revelation, partnership, action, and, at times, resistance.

From the time I entered EMT school until the year 2000, I had been following God's call in my career in EMS. As I stated in Chapter 1 "Following Your Heart", I had considered in my younger years becoming a missionary. Little did I know these two callings would soon intersect. As a youth in my church, I met some missionaries and learned about their experiences in other countries spreading the gospel of Jesus Christ. It was here God first placed the idea and the desire in me to go on my own missionary journey. As I grew older and finished high school, His calling and path had propelled me toward my EMS career. I had almost forgotten about the possibility of ever going on a missionary journey, but God had other plans.

One Sunday, a local physician and his wife came to our church seeking sponsorship and support for a two-week medical mission trip to West Africa. This was an opportunity for them to meet some medical needs and open the door to witness about the miracles of Jesus Christ. That spark inside my heart that God planted many years before began to grow. After the service I spoke with Dr. Atchley about the mission and asked if he could use my skills as a paramedic on his team, and he was excited that I was interested. I told him I would need to speak with my wife and pray about it more before my final decision, but we both agreed to continue in prayer and see where God would lead us.

My wife and I spent time in discussion and prayer, and Dr. Atchley provided us with the logistics and details of the two-week mission trip. We both agreed I should follow God's calling and pursue this opportunity to use my medical skills to witness to others. As a team, we spent the next several months gathering supplies, obtaining our passports, getting our vaccinations, and getting to know each other better. My church agreed to sponsor my flight and travel expenses to enable me to go on the trip. Our team would consist of Dr. Atchley, three nurses, a student ministry assistant, and myself. Our plan was to travel to the small country of Benin, in West Africa and, once there, we would meet with two local Baptist missionaries who had been living there for many years. They had secured a compound in a small village where we could stay, and they would be our guides and contacts during our time there.

Our travel to Benin was scheduled for October 2001 and we planned to set up basecamp in this village near where the missionaries lived. We intended to travel each day to different villages in the area, setting up clinics to treat those who were sick or injured. We also planned to provide the local people with vitamins for widespread malnutrition, and antimalarial drugs since that disease was so prevalent in the area. Moreover, the missionaries and some local pastors they had trained would have the opportunity to share the gospel with those who had been treated in our clinic.

Dr. Atchley's plan was for us to have one nurse perform triage and intake of patients, the second nurse run our makeshift pharmacy with the help of the ministry aid, the third nurse manage one exam area and treat patients, and Dr. Atchley manage the other exam area. My assignment was to assist in both exam rooms with procedures and treatments as necessary. We had a solid strategy and had acquired five large trunks of supplies, medical equipment, and medications and, by the end of August 2001, we were ready to go.

Of course, all of us who are old enough will never forget what transpired on September 11, 2001, when violent extremists attacked the United States, killing innocent civilians at the World Trade Center, the Pentagon, and on United Airlines Flight 93. This brutal attack changed all our lives forever. It certainly changed our plans to travel to Benin in October. Our entire team prayed about what we should do. We spoke with the missionaries and the Baptist Foreign Mission Board and, after careful consideration, we decided to delay our mission. We would change our plans and travel in March 2002.

Once March arrived, we were ready to fly from Atlanta to Paris, and then on to Cotonou, the largest city in Benin. At this point in my life, I had never flown on a commercial airline. I do not recommend your first trip be a total of 16 hours on a plane. We made it safely to the small airfield in Cotonou before daylight and worked our way through their security and customs run by their national military personnel. We had to answer a lot of questions about our equipment but, luckily, the missionaries had arranged a local leader to help us through the red tape without the authorities confiscating any of our equipment or medications. We began loading our equipment only to find that the trunk containing some of our surgical supplies and instruments had been placed on the wrong plane in Paris, and we would not receive it for a few days. Luckily, we had the foresight to not put all our like items in the same trunk, so we would have enough to get by for a couple of days without the missing equipment.

We met the local missionaries, loaded our equipment in a couple of Toyota pickup trucks, and traveled to the small house and compound where we would establish our base camp and get some rest from traveling. The next morning, we went to a local church service in a thatch and mud hut, and the remainder of the day was spent settling in and organizing our supplies for our daily clinics. That second night sleeping in the house was far from restful. We were in strange surroundings, it was exceptionally humid with no air conditioning, the beds were uncomfortable, and we struggled with the complete disruption to our normal sleep patterns from the time change. On top of my restless sleep, I unfortunately had a very vocal rooster that established himself outside my bedroom window. His clock was apparently off as well because he began to sound the alarm at 4 am, a good two hours before daylight.

At daylight we began to get ready. We quickly ate breakfast so that we could load up the pickup trucks and head out to our first village. As we traveled the dusty dirt roads in the back of the trucks through the countryside, we attracted quite a bit of attention wherever we traveled. We were stopped along the route by soldiers who required a "toll" for us to pass. It does test your faith to be sitting in the back of a pickup in a third world country facing soldiers with AK47's and not understanding what they are saying to the interpreter. This would not be the last time we would encounter such an impromptu check-point during our time in Benin, but fortunately we were allowed to pass safely each time.

Once we arrived in the first village, we set up our clinic in a small hut and hung some sheets to create privacy for the exam areas. It was a far cry from the nice medical facilities each of us were accustomed to working in, and it was a huge adjustment for us all. It was probably a little easier for me as a paramedic, as I was more accustomed to working in the elements and having to adapt and overcome environmental limitations. We had a long line of patients that entire day and, in 8 hours, we saw over 100 patients with an array of general complaints. These ranged from back pain to unhealed wounds, to malnourished infants, to HIV patients. The missionaries and local pastors shared the Gospel with each of these patients, and several accepted Christ and said they would begin attending the nearest church services. It was a long and exhausting day by the time we loaded up and traveled back to our compound, but we were invigorated and excited about what we had accomplished and looked forward to our other clinics.

In all, we visited 10 different villages during our time in Benin, and in each one there were hundreds of people we were able to treat and witness to. We cleaned wounds, performed a few minor surgeries, provided some much-needed medication to some very sick and malnourished children, and we even treated a young man who had an unfortunate encounter with a forest cobra. The word spread quickly about what we were doing, so much so that one day in one of the larger villages we were almost overrun by a huge crowd. I had to go into the crowd with a translator and triage who would get to be examined by the doctor, as the crowd was so large there was no way we could see them all in a single day.

On another day, we traveled north to one of the more remote villages we would visit during our trip. This village sat on the other side of a large river and had no road access. It would require us to leave the convenience of our trucks and load our equipment trunks in small dugout canoes called pirogues. There were several villagers who met us on the near shore to paddle us across the swift waters of the river. I traveled across with two of the trunks, guided by a young man who was maybe 16 years old. We loaded the trunks in the boat and my guide handed me an old coffee can. I immediately had a sinking (pun intended) suspicion of what the can was for. As I stepped into the small canoe, it was barely wide enough for my skinny frame, much less the trunks of equipment. We had not even left the shore yet and my feet were in a small puddle. So, with the coffee can in one hand and a small paddle in the other, we set out across the river, yet another test of faith.

We safely reached the other side and unloaded our equipment. While doing so, our interpreter told us this village has people killed each year from hippo attacks. I immediately thanked him for the heads-up now that we were already across the river.

Wooden Pirogue, Benin, West Africa 2002

It was in this village that I met the patient who sticks most in my mind. A grandmother brought us her extremely malnourished grandson who was about 18 months old; his body size and weight were much closer to the anticipated size of a three-month-old child. He was extremely frail, and his grandmother proceeded to tell us the boy's father had died of AIDS, and the mother was near death with the same illness and unable to care for the child. The child had been tested in Porto Novo and, by some miracle, was not HIV-positive. They had been trying to give the baby as much nourishment as possible by using a "wet nurse" in the mother's place. However, the poor nutrition of the entire area, and the fact the wet nurse had her own infant to feed, left little for this child. We did have a few cans of infant formula with us for such a situation. We arranged through the missionaries to get them more formula and to try to find a better option to enhance this little one's chances at survival. I held the frail little boy for quite some time, reflecting it had not been but a few years since I held my own frail child who had been fighting for his own life. Due to the compassion I had for this child I wanted to take him home with me, but I knew that was not possible and that this grandmother deeply loved her grandchild. That moment has profoundly stuck with me. The missionaries were able to keep track of the boy for a couple of years but, eventually, the grandmother and boy moved on, and we lost track. I often wonder what became of him.

It was amazing to be part of a team of healthcare providers who had never worked together, much less functioned in this strange environment while under less-than-desirable conditions. Despite our obstacles, we still made a difference in so many lives. We were able to meet some medical needs but, more importantly, we met some spiritual needs and saw many people accept Christ. It is a time in my life I will always cherish and a group of people I will never forget.

God has a calling and a purpose for each of us. For some it is a singular calling, and for others there can be multiple purposes or missions. For me and my life, I have been fortunate enough that my calling not only aligned with my professional career, but the other callings in my life intersected with each other. The medical mission to Benin is one example of where the talents God had given me, and the purpose for which He created me, allowed me to answer His call and serve others in multiple ways.

Each of us as individuals must be ever searching for the path God has laid out for us. We must be practicing and polishing the talents He has given us so that we are ready to use them for His purpose, and prepared to serve not only God but also our fellow man. Our calling by God may be singular throughout our entire life, or we may complete a God-given mission and He may give us a new assignment. You may be like me, and your multiple callings may occur simultaneously and be intersectional. Our job is to be close enough to God, and in daily communication with Him, to hear Him when He speaks and tells us the path to follow. We must be willing and ready to go forward and do good things, serving others and giving God all the glory. When that spiritual phone rings, we must answer the call.

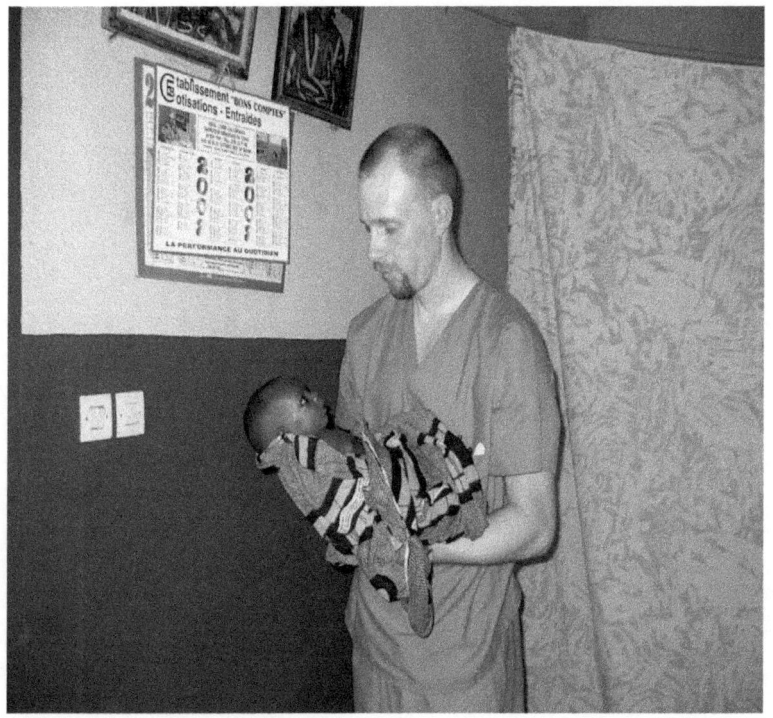

Brad with malnourished infant. Benin, West Africa 2002

CHAPTER 19

Finishing Strong

"Do you not know that those who run in a race all run, but one receives the prize? Run in such a way that you may obtain it." 1 Corinthians 9:24 NKJV

In this verse Paul is not speaking of a physical race, but a spiritual one. He is speaking to the church at Corinth, teaching them the importance of using their gifts in service to God and witnessing to others. This race is to win souls to Christ that they may receive salvation and eternal life, the ultimate prize in the race of life which, at some point, will end for us all. As I have mentioned throughout this book, we each were created and gifted to fulfill a God-given purpose.

Like running in an actual race, there will be times when you grow tired and weary. You may even feel like quitting, but you know you must finish the race. It is in those times we feel weak that we must tap into the strength and resolve of God. I know God has placed me in my position for a reason and no one wants to fail God, especially when lives are on the line.

The voice of fear and anxiousness is not the voice of God. One of the songs I sing while leading worship at my church with our band "Lift Him UP" is by Zach Williams, entitled "Fear is a Liar". The first verse and chorus say this: "When he told you you're not good enough. When he told you you're not right. When he told you you're not strong enough to put up a good fight. When he told you you're not worthy. When he told you you're not loved. When he told you you're not beautiful, you'll never be enough. Fear, he is a liar."

When you hear a voice telling you that you are falling behind in the race and someone else is beating you, you must realize it is the voice of defeat and not that of God. We are each running our own race and we are only competing against the person we were yesterday. If we are constantly walking with God, we can be confident we are exactly where we need to be. The enemy wants us to be distracted and jealous, focused on what others around us are doing instead of what God would have us do.

We have all probably met someone who constantly brags about their achievements, their successes, in life and in business. They typically do this to try to impress people or to make others feel inferior. They rarely share any of their failures or mistakes, and will even go to great lengths to hide them or to shift the blame to others. These are the types of people I do my best to avoid and from whom I try to distance myself. When I was younger and less mature, I was guilty of this myself at times. While I have had some success in my life, I hope you have discerned while reading this book that it is much more about what God has taught me through those lessons of life. I aspire each day to be better than I was the day before, to be closer to God than I was yesterday. I stray off course, get tired, face adversity, but continue to run the race for the crown.

As we each venture down the path to find our purpose, we each should be trying to learn and grow into the person God would have us to be. If anyone knows we are not perfect, it is God. That's why He sent His only Son, Jesus, to die for our imperfections. As we walk through this life, God is trying to refine us and mold us into the creation He designed. Well-known strategist, speaker, and author Myron Golden concluded, "Every difficult thing that you have ever had to overcome in life was ordained by and approved by God to make you strong enough for the thing He created you for." I agree that God uses challenges and difficulties to make us stronger. He knows there will be times when we fail, but He also knows that if we acknowledge those failures and learn from them, they will shape us into the person He would have us to be. We can become an improved product from those mistakes and not allow those failures to define who we are.

Whether you best serve your calling within the church and its missions or if, like me, your calling has aligned with your profession, it is important for us to seek God's direction and guidance to find the right path. For me, being a paramedic and a leader has been a lifelong calling. I assure you it has not always been easy and not every person can do it. Most will not be successful for very long without being gifted and called to do this work. I have faced many struggles, trials, and tribulations while following God. I have walked through countless strangers' tragedies during their most difficult days and been expected to be calm and perform at my best. None of it would have been possible for me to endure, much less thrive, if God had not been with me each step of the way.

I hope after reading this book you comprehend that I sought to fill my heart with God-given principles. Then, as my heart aligned with His plan, I followed it down the path toward my purpose. Along the way, it required compassion to others and to myself. There were times the seeds of complacency sprouted in my garden and yielded fruits of mediocrity. As I grew and leaned more on God and His power, I began to gain more confidence and learned to be calm under pressure. God's strength gave me the ability to be bold and stand up for what is right. He enabled me to be brave in the face of danger or persecution. As I continually tried to walk Gods path, He was faithful to walk with me and light the way when it became dark or obscured. He continued to reveal His vision for my life and how I could use the gifts He had given me. He placed Godly people in my life who used their talents to coach, hold me accountable, listen to my problems, give Godly advice, and fight for me when I faced opposition. God continued to mold and shape me, teaching me to be firm and stand on His principles. He taught me to be fair in my dealings with others and show the same grace He showed me. God instilled in me the gift of assertiveness and a desire to serve, which enabled me to step up and fill gaps when needed. In following His principles and reading His Examples from the Bible, I obtained the discernment to know when to lead from the front, guide from the middle, or guard the backs of my people.

God most definitely walked with me through many dark days but, by His strength and power, He turned them into defining moments. When my burdens became heavy, God gave me strength and sent talented people to help support me. He sowed a seed in me that, over time, He nurtured and allowed to grow into a mature plant, which consequently enabled me to yield my own seeds to sow. God helped me tame my tongue and was quick to convict and correct me when I wielded my sword recklessly. He guided me to ask forgiveness from those I harmed. As I began to yield my own fruits and invest in others, He increased the harvest and gave a return on that investment. When I faced struggles and had questions, God was always faithful to answer if I was dedicated enough to ask, seek, and knock. God has opened many doors for me, and I have attempted to honor Him in all I have done and continue to do. All the glory and honor go to Him for all He has done in me and through me.

As you walk your path and run your race, my prayer is you will seek God's guidance and direction. My desire is that, while you have read through my reflections and the lessons God has taught me, you have been able to draw something useful from it. It is my sincere wish that it has drawn you to seek and know God if you have never had a relationship with Him. If you are already a Christian, I hope this has brought you some encouragement or has revealed areas in your own life that God can help strengthen and refine. If you picked up this book because you are trying to find the path God would have you walk, I am optimistic it will shine a light on your purpose. If you are an EMS professional, or work in any public safety profession, my intent has been to honor the work that countless brave men and women do 24/7/365. The one true way to be satisfied and happy is through selfless service to others, and that is the embodiment of EMS.

We follow God's call to serve our fellow man and honor Him. That is what I have spent my entire life doing, and will continue to do for as long as God needs me. Will it always be at the same place and in the same position? Only God knows. I started this writing journey as a self-reflection, seeking God's guidance for the next phase of my life. Throughout this process, He has continued to reveal lessons to me and draw me even closer to Him. Can I say, as I near completion of this book, that I have God's definitive answer regarding whether and when I should retire from my position at JCEMS and move to the next assignment He has for me? I cannot. I do know He has revealed several areas in which I still need work. One of the songs I used to sing in the children's choir at church says, "He's still working on me". I am confident that God still has a use for my gifts and still wants me to serve others, mentor leaders, and minister in my church. I know God is faithful and will continue to lay His path before me until my time on Earth is done. I also know it will require me to be continually seeking His presence, and diligently following Him every single day, and I pray you realize He desires the same relationship with you.

If you have made it this far, you have taken some positive steps on your journey to find and fulfill your purpose. I encourage you to keep running your race toward the finish line. Along the way, follow your heart, find compassion, fight complacency, be bold and brave, be firm but flexible, and be fair and forgiving. Know that you do not run alone, that God is with you and will give you strength and confidence. When the race seems hard and you want to quit, turn to God and He will ease your burden. As you travel your path, sow the seeds God has given you on fertile ground so that He may reap a bountiful harvest. Run your race in service to others, for it is the conduit to true happiness. I pray you discover your destined direction, and that you follow it. Find and fulfill your purpose and finish strong.

Riding on the Jefferson County Sheriff Department MRAP

"As a prisoner for the Lord, then, I urge you to live a life worthy of the calling you have received. Be completely humble and gentle; be patient, bearing with one another in love. Make every effort to keep the unity of the Spirit through the bond of peace."

Ephesians 4: 1-3 NIV

www.ingramcontent.com/pod-product-compliance
Lightning Source LLC
LaVergne TN
LVHW011417080426
835512LV00005B/104